What people Are

Pantheon: Th

In the pursuit of a mystic spirituality, finding a trustworthy and perceptive teacher is essential. Enter author Laura Perry with her recent work, *Pantheon: The Minoans*. Perry's clear writing, thorough historical research, and insightful spiritual observations serve as a guiding light for all magical practitioners. Every skill level is welcome here. *Pantheon: The Minoans* starts off as a concise tour through Minoan history and culture as well as a survey of the many faces of the divine. But *Patheon* isn't some librarian's info-dump. Like the mythic Ariadne, Perry's work acts as your guide, leading you through the labyrinth towards a treasure trove of Minoan spiritual practices. The book generously offers step-by-step instructions to the core celebratory and magical formats that have inspired and informed Ariadne's Tribe, an inclusive modern polytheistic spiritual tradition. Although intended as an introduction, *Pantheon: The Minoans* is far more significant and impactful. It's a revelation for anyone who has wondered about modern Minoan spirituality, the deities, feasts, myths, and magic, and how one might engage with their own powerful practice.
Timothy Roderick, author of *Wicca: A Year and A Day*, *Dark Moon Mysteries*, and other works

Pantheon: The Minoans is a fascinating guide to Minoan paganism and culture which is perfect for anyone interested in Minoan beliefs or who is just curious about the culture. The author tackles what can be a complicated subject in a way that makes it easy for readers. Covering all the essentials from deities to holidays, from history to ritual structure, in a straightforward way. This book deserves a place in any witch's library.

Morgan Daimler, author of *Pantheon: The Norse*

Laura Perry has succeeded in the most needed task of compiling authentic references and explanations for the old gods of this very misunderstood culture and region. Ancient Minoan religion is something that still perplexes scholars to this day so having a trusted reference point for these old gods is a great boon for practicing polytheists and researchers alike.

David Salisbury, author of *The Deep Heart of Witchcraft*

This is a fascinating book, offering insight into the history, culture and religions of not just Minoan Crete, but the ancient Mediterranean as a whole. While it's aimed at people who want to practice modern Minoan spirituality, the book has a lot to offer readers like myself who are simply drawn to the historical side. I very much enjoyed it.

Nimue Brown, author of *Druidry and Meditation*, *Druidry and the Ancestors*, and *Pagan Dreaming*

Laura Perry takes us back in time to the ancient world of the Minoans. This magical book reveals the history, culture, and ways of these mysterious people who have influenced the Mediterranean and brought powerful deities back to us. Each page teaches us how to create a spiritual practice that summons the Minoans to help us to connect to a culture that was an enigma until now.

Chris Allaun, author of *Whispers from the Coven*

Pantheon: The Minoans is a fascinating walk through the history and the magical tradition of what we know about the Minoan people and their culture. It also explores the identities the deities within this tradition and what they represented to the people. Laura Perry explains how this tradition can be practiced successfully in modern times. She is the Temple Mom of Ariadne's Tribe and has been working on this spiritual path as a community effort for about a decade. Her research into uncovering the Minoans' real identity and the Gods and Goddesses that were worshiped gives a clearer understanding of the origins of these deities and how over the centuries they have made their way into other pantheons, particularly the Greeks. It is an enjoyable piece and well worth the read.

Martha Gray, author of *Grimalkyn: The Witch's Cat*

Laura Perry's *Pantheon: The Minoans* is the perfect introduction to understanding and celebrating all things Cretan. Written with expertise and dedication, Laura guides the reader into developing an ever deepening and insightful relationship with the Minoan deities. Using reconstructionist methods developed with her highly successful Ariadne's Tribe group, along with archaeological and comparative mythology. Laura's expertise and dedication shine through her writing, which is both instructive and engaging. By the end of the book, the reader will understand the everyday lives of the Minoans and how they celebrated the seasons. This is especially evident in the Sacred Calander chapter which reveals how the seasonal changes in the Mediterranean area were totally in tune with both the harvests and the Minoan people's religious practices in Bronze Age Crete. In short, this book is a treasure trove of knowledge and history. With Laura as your teacher, you cannot fail to cultivate a profound and rewarding relationship with the Minoan Pantheon.

Thea Prothero, author of *A Guide to Pilgrimage*

Pantheon:
The Minoans

Pantheon: The Minoans

Laura Perry

MOON BOOKS
London, UK
Washington, DC, USA

CollectiveInk

First published by Moon Books, 2025
Moon Books is an imprint of Collective Ink Ltd.,
Unit 11, Shepperton House, 89 Shepperton Road, London, N1 3DF
office@collectiveinkbooks.com
www.collectiveinkbooks.com
www.moon-books.net

For distributor details and how to order please visit the 'Ordering' section on our website.

A CIP catalogue record for this book is available from the British Library.

Design: Lapiz Digital Services

UK: Printed and bound by CPI Group (UK) Ltd, Croydon, CR0 4YY
Printed in North America by CPI GPS partners

Contents

Previous Titles

Ariadne's Thread: Awakening the Wonders of the
Ancient Minoans in Our Modern Lives
second edition, ISBN 979-8393342753.

Labrys & Horns: An Introduction to Modern Minoan Paganism
second edition, ISBN 979-8648863491.

The Minoan Coloring Book
second edition, ISBN 978-1702811286.

The Minoan Tarot
ISBN 978-0764352317.

To the family of deities and humans who make up
Ariadne's Tribe.
Together we are joy!

Acknowledgements

This book, like so many other works about spirituality, is the culmination of a long-term collaborative process within a community. That community is Ariadne's Tribe. I'm grateful to all the Tribe members who have participated in the conversations and research that helped build our spiritual tradition. I'm especially indebted to our other board members, Dana Corby, Bryan Hewitt, and Arlechina Verdigris, for helping to turn an online discussion group into a fully-formed and inclusive spiritual tradition. My gratitude also goes to Trevor Greenfield and the other great people at Moon Books and Collective Ink. In a world where the publishing industry is increasingly a minefield for authors, Trevor has maintained a supportive and collaborative environment, for which I'm grateful. And as always, my thanks to Ray and Sky, for filling my life with love.

Introduction

This book is an introduction to the ancient Minoans and their family of deities as well as the spiritual practices of Ariadne's Tribe, a worldwide inclusive modern polytheistic spiritual tradition. The information in these pages is aimed at people who don't already have much background knowledge about the Minoans and their religion but who are interested in learning. It's important to understand any culture's place in history if you want to understand their religious beliefs and practices. That information gives us the context for bringing their spirituality alive in the modern world. So I've included details about ancient Minoan religion and daily life along with the Tribe's modern sacred calendar and ritual structure, which are based on the information we have available about Minoan religion.

The Minoans were a literate society, but the script they used to write their language, called Linear A, is still undeciphered. So we don't have any Minoan texts to help us out. The modern Minoan spiritual tradition I've shared in these pages is built on a combination of reconstructionist techniques (archaeology, archaeoastronomy, dance ethnology and comparative mythology) plus shared gnosis, since the historical resources are limited and there are lots of blanks to fill in. Throughout the book, I've explained where we've used our own spiritual experiences to flesh out the available information and when specific types of research, like dance ethnology or archaeoastronomy, have been important. We've done our best to remain true to what we know about the Minoans from reliable sources while also maintaining a functional and meaningful spiritual practice as modern Pagans.

Ariadne's Tribe, or "the Tribe" for short, is a worldwide inclusive spiritual tradition. This means that people of any race, ethnicity, gender, sexual orientation, ability level, disability, geographic location, language, education, or socio-economic status are welcome. We're open to everyone who shares our love for the Minoan deities and respect for our fellow human beings. We're not affiliated with any other Minoan-themed spiritual tradition.

Some of the material in this book first appeared, with slightly different wording, on my Minoan Path blog on PaganSquare at WitchesAndPagans.com. This book isn't long enough to go in depth into any of the aspects of Minoan religion and history that I touch on in the blog. I've included what I consider to be the most important information for a basic understanding of ancient Minoan culture and religion and modern Minoan spirituality.

I hope you'll take advantage of the resources I've listed at the end of the book. The Glossary provides information about terms you may not be familiar with. And the Further Reading section, as well as the bibliography if you're so inclined, can help you explore the subjects found in this book in greater depth. I'd also like to mention here that I wrote this book myself, without the aid of text-generating AI. I dislike having to include this kind of announcement, but here we are.

The Minoans were real people, ordinary people just like us. They had families and jobs. They traveled and farmed and herded. They worshiped at home and in temples and shrines. They laughed and cried and loved. And they saw the divine in the world around them. We can connect with those deities in the modern world, just as the Minoans did in their time. This book is a great place to start making that connection.

Chapter 1

The Minoans in History

If we want to understand ancient Minoan religion and bring their pantheon into our modern spiritual practice, we need to know about the Minoans as human beings. Who were they? When did they live, and how did they live? What were they like?

Let's start with a more basic subject: their name. Believe it or not, the people of ancient Crete didn't call themselves *Minoan*. Ancient Egyptian sources call them "Keftiu," and they may be the "Caphtor" mentioned in the Old Testament of the Christian Bible. So where did the term *Minoan* come from?

Sir Arthur Evans was the British archaeologist who excavated Knossos in the early 20th century. A few people had suggested the term "Minoan" before he came along, but it didn't stick. Evans wanted to prove the Greek myths were historically true, and he thought the temple at Knossos was King Minos's palace. So he called the people "Minoan" after the king's name. Evans's relentless PR campaign to make sure the whole world knew about his work immortalized the name, and it's been with us ever since. Maybe one day we'll discover the word the Minoans used to describe themselves. But for now, we'll just call them Minoan.

Some other ideas Evans had about the Minoans turned out to be completely wrong. Evans was proud to be a part of the British Empire, which he considered the height of civilization. So when he found an ancient "high civilization" on Crete, he figured it must have had the same hallmarks as the British Empire: monarchy, military, and monotheism. Although Evans's theories were popular in his day, since then, archaeologists have concluded they're incorrect. Sadly, Evans's outdated theories continue to circulate online, despite archaeologists' attempts to share more updated information with the public.

To begin with, there's no credible evidence the Minoans ever had a monarchy. It appears that each city on Crete was governed by a small group of temple clergy and possibly lay people as well. But Evans believed there was a monarchy, so he called the temple in Knossos a palace and named its rooms according to the way he imagined the royal family used them: the king's Throne Room, the Queen's Megaron, and so on. Archaeologists now generally agree that the famous Throne Room, with its central stone seat flanked by big griffins painted on the wall, was a ritual room and not a royal audience chamber.

There's also no evidence of a military on Crete before the Mycenaean occupation, and during the occupation, the military belonged to the Mycenaeans (early Greeks from the mainland to the north of Crete), not the Minoans. Don't panic; I'll explain the Mycenaean occupation a little further down in this chapter. A lot of archaeologists think the Minoans had a merchant marine to protect their trading fleets. It's possible, though there's no real evidence one way or the other. It's clear the Minoans put all their extensive resources into trade instead of conquest.

The "goddess monotheism" that Evans did his best to prove turns out to be wrong as well. The Minoans didn't worship a single Great Goddess to the exclusion of other deities. Like all the other Bronze Age cultures in and around the Mediterranean, the Minoans were polytheists.

That's a lot of stuff the Minoans *weren't*. So what were they? And who were they? They were a Bronze Age culture centered on the island of Crete in the Mediterranean Sea, just south of mainland Greece. They weren't Greek, but they did influence the Mycenaeans a lot.

Crete is the largest of the islands that belong to the modern nation of Greece, but it has only been a part of Greece for just over a century, since 1913. The island is long and narrow, about

260 km (160 miles) wide from east to west and 60 km (37 miles) across from north to south in the middle, narrowing toward both ends. The center of the island is filled with a mountain range that forms a sort of "spine" running east to west along the island's length. These mountains, many of which were sacred to the Minoans, are surrounded by fertile lowlands crisscrossed by rivers. The mild climate made Crete a desirable place to live in Minoan times, just as it is today.

The Mediterranean climate has a unique seasonal cycle. I'll explain it briefly here, because being familiar with it will help you understand the Minoan sacred calendar, which is based on Crete's natural cycles. If you're reading this book, there's a good chance you live in the northern temperate zone with its four seasons of spring, summer, autumn, and winter. But in the Mediterranean, there are only two seasons: rainy and dry. The rains begin in the autumn, which is when the farmers plow their fields and plant their crops. The grain and vegetables grow through the mild, rainy winter and are harvested in the spring. So the times for planting and harvest may be backward from what you're used to. Once the harvest is over, the springtime moves into summer, and the rains stop. In the Mediterranean, the "dead time" is the summer, not the winter. It's very hot and completely dry. The rivers on Crete become shallow and sluggish; many streams dry up entirely. Plants turn brown and crispy. There's no relief until the rains begin again in the autumn, starting a new cycle.

Let's look at the basic timeline of events to help us get an idea of where the Minoans fit into the big picture of history. They didn't just appear out of nowhere in the Bronze Age. DNA evidence tells us the Minoans' ancestors migrated to the Aegean from Anatolia (modern-day Turkey) during the Neolithic era, around 10,000 to 9000 BCE. Theirs was only one of many waves of migration out of Anatolia into Europe and the Mediterranean as populations swelled with the introduction of farming. These migrants were part of Old Europe, the people who were there before the Indo-Europeans arrived.

The first settlements on Crete were in caves, then farmsteads and small villages. Slowly over time the population grew. Villages became towns and towns became cities. By around 3500 to 3000 BCE, the art and culture looked recognizably Minoan. By then, the Minoans were already sailing around the Mediterranean, building their trading empire. But they still didn't have the big temples and gleaming cities that have captured our imaginations.

The temples in the major Minoan cities of Knossos, Phaistos, Malia, and Zakros were all built around 1900 BCE. Those temples, which are still sometimes wrongly referred to as palaces, held a complex and important role in Minoan society. Like the temples in ancient Mesopotamia, the Minoan ones were centers for both religious activities and local government. Each city and its surrounding farmland were governed from the temple. Crete didn't have a unified island-wide government. Instead, the Minoan cities were united by their culture and religion, which they all shared.

The temples were the crowning glory of the Minoan cities, which were pretty advanced for their time, especially compared to other nearby cultures. The Minoans built aqueducts to bring water into their cities from the mountain springs. Their temples and many of their homes had piped-in fresh water, indoor toilets, and sewer systems. Their city streets were paved, with gutters along the edges for runoff. Their level of sanitation must have improved their health considerably.

I mentioned that the big temples were built around 1900 BCE. About 200 years later the temples, along with the cities that surrounded them, were damaged by devastating earthquakes and had to be rebuilt. Minoan architecture was remarkably earthquake-resistant, so much so that modern architects have studied the remains of Minoan buildings to help them make contemporary buildings more earthquake-proof.

Earthquakes are a common hazard in the Mediterranean, which has active geology that includes volcanoes. You can probably guess where this is going. Around 1600 BCE, the volcanic island of Thera erupted catastrophically in the eastern Mediterranean, blowing a big hole in its own center and sending earthquakes, tsunamis, and an enormous ash cloud across the whole region. The tsunamis scoured the northern and eastern coasts of Crete, destroying the cities and temples there.

A century ago, archaeologists thought the Thera eruption was the end of Minoan civilization. But newer scientific evidence shows that the eruption happened one to two centuries earlier than people originally thought, and the Minoans rebuilt afterward. As you can imagine, their island was seriously damaged by the natural disaster, and that set the stage for the Mycenaeans to take advantage. The Mycenaeans weren't related to the Minoans. They were an Indo-European people who came into mainland Greece during the early Bronze Age in one of the waves of Indo-European migration that swept westward from the Pontic-Caspian steppe, a region of grasslands in eastern Europe and western Asia.

We don't know exactly how it happened, whether the Mycenaeans offered to help in a friendly manner to start with or whether they were more forceful right from the beginning. But by about a century after the Thera eruption, they had fully taken over at Knossos and were also overseeing the activities at Phaistos and possibly at Chania, in western Crete, as well. But they never managed to take over at Malia, Zakros, or the other cities on the eastern end of the island. This era, the last two to three centuries of Minoan civilization, is called the Mycenaean occupation of Crete. It's during this time the Mycenaeans learned so much about Minoan culture and borrowed a number of Minoan deities into their pantheon. The later classical Greeks (Hellenes) inherited these borrowed deities, which is how so many Minoan deities ended up in the Hellenic pantheon.

5

Sadly, it appears that when the Minoans continued to resist Mycenaean rule, the Mycenaeans responded viciously. Around 1450 BCE, all the major cities along the northern and eastern coast of Crete (except Knossos, where the Mycenaeans had their headquarters) were systematically looted and burned to the ground, if not by the Mycenaeans themselves, then possibly by their hired mercenaries. This is why we have very little in the way of precious metal artifacts from the Minoans, even though they were very wealthy. The looters removed anything of value and most likely melted down all the gold and silver items they could find.

Knossos continued under Mycenaean rule for another century. Then, around 1350 BCE, it, too, was looted and burned to the ground. We don't know for certain who was responsible, but one reasonable possibility involves the native Minoans who had fled their burning cities a century earlier. After the destruction of their cities, many of them holed up in communities like Karphi in the mountains of east central Crete, remote strongholds of resistance against the Mycenaean occupation. Maybe they'd simply had enough.

Believe it or not, even after all this destruction, there were still people living on Crete. The island wasn't empty. But without the big cities and their infrastructure, daily life was more difficult. It became even more so as the eastern Mediterranean plunged into the Late Bronze Age (LBA) collapse, which peaked (or bottomed out, I suppose you could say) around 1100 BCE. By that point, governments had failed, trade was endangered by pirates, and people were struggling simply to survive. The LBA collapse was due to a combination of causes including climate change, drought, famine, civil unrest, and governmental instability.

This is the end of the Minoan era. Beyond this point, there's no art or architecture that's recognizably Minoan. The people of Crete continued on, of course. They didn't all just disappear. Crete continued to be inhabited through the Hellenic and

Roman eras, right up until today. But by the time of the LBA collapse, Minoan civilization was gone for good.

How can we place the Minoans on our mental map of the ancient world? They flourished at the same time as other ancient cultures you're probably already familiar with. They interacted with many different people around the Mediterranean, including the Egyptians, who were one of their major trading partners.

How do the Minoans dovetail with ancient Egyptian history? The Old Kingdom in Egypt began in about 3100 BCE, just a few centuries after the culture on Crete became recognizably Minoan. The height of Minoan civilization happened around the same time as many of the big names you're probably familiar with in Egyptian history: Hatshepsut, Akhenaten, Nefertiti, Tutankhamun. But the Egyptians weren't the only people around at that time.

In Mesopotamia, Sumerian culture arose at about the same time as early Minoan civilization. A few centuries later, while the Minoans were expanding their cities, Sargon of Akkad conquered the Sumerian city-states and united them to form the Akkadian Empire. Then the Babylonian Empire arose in the same region. King Hammurabi with his famous laws lived about the same time the Minoans were building their first big temples.

We've already mentioned the Mycenaeans. These early Greeks appeared as a culture during the last few centuries of Minoan civilization, and their rise is attributed largely to the Minoans. From the Minoans they learned how to build beehive-shaped tombs, how to write, how to improve their sailing ships, bronze, pottery and jewelry-making. But unlike the Minoans, their culture was warlike and profited mainly from conquest instead of trade.

The Mycenaeans borrowed deities from the Minoan pantheon, adding them to their own religious practice. Dionysus, Eileithyia,

Rhea and others began in Minoan Crete but eventually made their way into Greek mythology. The fragments of their myths that survived into the classical era helped us find our way back to their earlier Minoan stories. You'll probably recognize many of the Minoan deity names because you've seen them in Greek myth and folk tales. Just be aware the Minoan deities don't necessarily have the same characteristics as the later Hellenic ones.

Along with the other Mediterranean and Near Eastern cultures, Mycenaean civilization fell apart during the LBA collapse. There was what you might call a dark age for a while, a time we don't have much information about. Classical Greek civilization didn't arise until several centuries after the collapse, when the Minoans and the Mycenaeans were both long gone.

What about other regions of the world? What was going on elsewhere while the Minoans were busy painting frescoes and leaping over bulls?

The first stage of Stonehenge was built during the early days of Minoan civilization, while the people of Crete were gathering in towns but before they began building their big temples. The final stage of rearranging stones and dirt at Stonehenge took place during the height of Minoan culture.

Like the Egyptians and Sumerians, the Minoans were also a literate culture. They wrote using two different scripts, Cretan hieroglyphs and Linear A. We don't have enough texts of either of them yet to be able to do a decipherment, unfortunately. But we can see from the surviving examples that the hieroglyphs were used on stone seals, and both hieroglyphs and Linear A were used in bookkeeping records in the temples and smaller sacred houses. Although we can't read the text, the numbers have been deciphered, and we can see the Minoans were confident mathematicians who used both whole numbers and unit fractions (fractions with a 1 in the numerator and another number in the denominator, like ½ or ¼). Archaeologists are still finding more Linear A texts, so maybe one day we'll have enough for a decipherment.

In the meantime, we can already read Linear B, a script based on Linear A and used at Knossos and several Mycenaean cities in mainland Greece. Both of these scripts were used to write on clay tablets about the size of your hand, which were used for bookkeeping and administration at the Minoan temples and other sites. But Linear B wasn't used to write the Minoan language. Instead, it was used to record the early form of Greek the Mycenaeans spoke. Since the Mycenaeans were illiterate until they met the Minoans, the Minoans probably developed Linear B for them. This may have happened under duress, since Linear B's appearance happened at the height of the Mycenaean occupation of Crete.

Enough Linear B texts have survived that it was deciphered in the middle of the 20th century. So we can read the Mycenaean Greek on those tablets. That may not sound too exciting, since they're accounting records. But the words on the tablets give us a glimpse into a hybrid Minoan-Mycenaean culture, including the names of deities, trade goods, occupations, and food. This information has helped us reconstruct a great deal about life on Crete at the end of the Minoan era.

The writing, the art, the paved roads and sewers and big temples the Minoans created are all pretty impressive. But what's most impressive is that Minoan culture lasted peacefully for so many centuries before finally succumbing to a combination of human and natural causes. Then the Minoans remained hidden from view for three millennia before being rediscovered by archaeologists at the turn of the twentieth century. Now that we know a little about their history, let's explore their religion and their worldview.

Chapter 2

The Minoan Worldview

We know when the Minoans lived and what their culture looked like. But how did they experience the world? What did they believe? We can understand a lot about the Minoan worldview based on the way they lived and worshiped. And we know about those things because archaeologists have uncovered the remains of Minoan cities, temples, cave shrines and mountain peak sanctuaries.

First, let me say that Minoan Crete wasn't a utopia. A lot of people look to the Minoans as some sort of idealized, near-perfect "golden age" past culture. But they were human, just like us. They had their problems and challenges. And the way they interacted with the world, both the material and the numinous, says a lot about them. Even if Minoan society wasn't a utopia, there are a lot of things we can learn from them that can help us make our own world a better place.

The art and archaeology of ancient Crete tell us the Minoans maintained Neolithic lifeways well into the Bronze Age. In other words, the practices and values their ancestors brought with them when they migrated south from Anatolia thousands of years earlier lived on in later Minoan culture. This worldview may seem radical compared to the way we live these days, especially in the West. But Dr. Marija Gimbutas's work has now been validated by hard archaeological evidence. So we know the Minoans lived in very much the same way the people of Old Europe and Neolithic Anatolia did: in a largely peaceful, non-militarized, non-monarchical society whose religious practices were polytheistic and animistic and included ancestor reverence.

The values that matrilineal societies have traditionally supported are a big part of the attraction of Minoan spirituality.

The Minoans appear to have prized egalitarianism, inclusion, interdependence, and an animistic reverence for nature. Those are among the major principles we espouse in Ariadne's Tribe. They inform our spiritual practice and our daily lives. They're enshrined in our Official Policies. And we do our best to be living examples of these values as we interact with the world at large. What might these values have looked like in Minoan Crete?

The Minoans appear not to have feared the dead the way so many other societies have long done. The earliest organized religious activities on Crete that we have evidence of involved the communal tombs the Minoans' ancestors used to bury their dead, first in caves and later in beehive-shaped buildings. These tombs had plazas in front of them where the people held seasonal communal feasts and made offerings to their beloved dead. Hundreds of cups used to make offerings have been found at these places.

The Minoans practiced secondary burial, which involves waiting until a body that has been laid out in the communal tomb has decayed down to just bones, then lovingly taking the skeleton apart and placing the bones in a larnax or pithos along with the bones of other family members. So they spent a great deal of time caring for their dead and celebrating them, probably alongside reverence for their deities.

In some parts of Crete, instead of using large tombs, the people continued the Neolithic practice of burying their beloved dead beneath the floor of the family home, keeping them close to maintain their kinship beyond death. Offerings to the dead, prayers to them, and to the deities on their behalf, would have been integral parts of daily life. Imagine how different life would be if you lived knowing you'd still be loved and cared for after death.

Even after the Minoans built their temples and cities, the values of interconnection and sharing continued. There's evidence of large public feasts at the temples, when the clergy shared food with the people. Whole rooms full of giant storage vessels contained excess grain, wine, and oil for these feasts and to share with the people in times of need. Coming from the temples, this practice of sharing and generosity would have been viewed as sacred, as if the food was coming from the deities themselves.

These values of sharing with others and caring for both the living and the dead derive from an animistic and polytheistic worldview and a set of ideals that anthropological research shows are typical for matrilineal societies. Like other such cultures, the Minoans would have seen the animals and plants and even the landscape features around them, the mountains and rivers, as their relatives, as inspirited and sacred. The archaeological evidence suggests the Minoans had what's called a gift economy or sharing economy, in which they valued the kinds of caring, generosity, and compassion that mothers extend to their children, or Mother Goddesses to theirs. This generosity extended from individual families to the temples and is still visible in the profound sense of hospitality and generosity the Cretan people show today.

The position of nature in Minoan religion is evident in the cave shrines and mountain peak sanctuaries they built as well as in the constant, vivid presence of nature in Minoan art. The Minoans made pilgrimages to these sacred places in nature, performing rituals and making offerings there. Many offering items, including small terracotta and bronze figurines, have been found at these sites. I'll go into more detail about offerings later on in this chapter. Some of the Minoan cave shrines continued in use well into the Christian era, and several mountain peaks on Crete are still considered sacred today.

"Nature" is more than just the plants, animals, and mountains, though. It's also the starry sky. Astronomy was a major aspect of Minoan religion. The temples, peak sanctuaries, and other buildings were all constructed with astronomical alignments to the sun, moon, planets, and stars. If you'd like more information about this fascinating subject, I recommend the Minoan Astronomy website of the Uppsala Archaeoastronomical Project, which contains the work of several archaeoastronomers from Uppsala University. They've generously uploaded copies of their peer-reviewed papers to make them accessible to the public.

The Minoans saw the divine in the cosmos as well as on their own island and in the Mediterranean sea around them. The times and places where those realms intersected, when the sun or moon or a particular planet or star rose above a sacred mountain peak or set beneath the waves would have been especially sacred.

What about the specifics of Minoan religion? What did they actually do in those temples and shrines? Minoan art offers us "snapshots" of ritual activity, and artifacts found at sacred sites give us more insight into the ways the Minoans practiced their religion. This includes ecstatic singing and dancing, trance possession, making offerings and libations, worshiping in front of shrines, standing in ritual ecstatic postures, holding dining rituals for the dead, and interacting with sacred stones and trees. Since all we have from the art is individual freeze-frame images of these rituals, we don't know the details of how these practices were performed. But what we can see is telling: the connection with nature, the openness to the presence of the divine, personal interaction with the deities and the ancestors, joy and ecstasy.

We can see from the art that the Minoans performed these activities in lots of different sacred spaces, from the temples and the tombs to the mountain peak sanctuaries, the sacred caves, outdoor shrines, and even simple home shrines. Although not many private homes have been excavated, the ones that have been examined show the Minoans had altars in their homes, in much the same way modern Pagans often do.

Another aspect of this worldview is that religion wasn't separate from the rest of life. Yes, the Minoans celebrated festival days with special events at the temples and other big sacred sites. But they also had altars and shrines in their homes and businesses. Like other Bronze Age people, they would have spent their lives constantly aware of the sacred around them and within them. There was no sacred-versus-mundane. It was all holy, all numinous, all infused with the divine.

All of this, the mountains, the caves, the stars, the ancestors, the temples, the people themselves, all of it was connected with the deities. So what we see with the Minoans, ultimately, is a culture that viewed the world as an interconnected web of being: alive, inspirited, and sacred. The deities are, perhaps, the ultimate expression of this concept. But everything else, the cities and the wilderness, the ancestors and the living, is also a part of that web.

As I mentioned above, one of the major aspects of Minoan religious practice, for people from all walks of life, involved making offerings. In a sense, this goes back to the concept of sharing, though in this case it's sharing with the deities. We have direct evidence of many types of offerings because archaeologists have dug up the items the Minoans gave to their deities. Of course, most biodegradable materials like food and drink will have long since decayed away. There is one exception, though. In the 1960s, archaeologist Nikolas Platon was excavating the temple in the Minoan city of Zakros, on the far eastern end of Crete. In one of the temple wells he found a conical cup full of olives. It had miraculously been preserved by the silt in the bottom of the well. Platon interpreted the cup as a "ritual deposit," in other words, an offering to the deities.

Although that dish of olives is unusual in terms of biodegradable offerings surviving the centuries, it does tell us the Minoans made offerings pretty much the same way all their neighbors did, giving food and drink as well as non-perishable items to their deities.

14

They often used special offering stands to place food on, and bowl-topped ones to pour libations into. Rhytons (ceremonial pitchers) were also popular. While some were simple jug and pitcher styles, others were made in animal shapes like birds and cattle, perhaps to evoke the deity the offering was for.

In terms of non-perishable offerings, hundreds of small figurines have been found at the Minoan cave shrines and peak sanctuaries, left there by devotees during the Bronze Age. These bronze and terracotta figurines often take human form, usually with the person in some kind of ritual posture like the Minoan salute, a pose in which the person curls their right hand into a loose fist then holds the back of the hand against the forehead. It's likely these were "portraits" of the people making the offering, maybe giving thanks for some gift they had received via the deity or simply offering their devotion.

Many other figurines are shaped like animals. These include cattle, goats, and dogs as well as more unusual ones like weasels and rhinoceros beetles. The livestock and dog figurines may have been offered in thanks for good health for the person's animal, or to ask for healing and protection for them. The weasels may have been the local method for keeping rodents out of stored grain. The beetles, well, we haven't quite figured them out yet!

The most unusual type of offering item found at Minoan sacred sites is body parts. I don't mean actual ones, of course, but little terracotta or bronze replicas. The finds from the peak sanctuaries and cave shrines include arms, legs, heads, and torsos. Archaeologists interpret these as offerings asking for healing for specific injuries or illnesses. These fascinating items may have been brought to the cave shrines and peak sanctuaries by the people who were seeking healing, or if they were too sick, maybe a family member or close friend made the pilgrimage for them to seek the deity's aid. It's also possible that at least some of them represented constellations in the night sky.

The deities, then, were at the center of it all. They're the reason the Minoans built those enormous temples and dedicated all those peak sanctuaries and cave shrines. The deities are the ones the people made their offerings to, asking for help or giving thanks, and the ones they built shrines and altars for, in their homes and other spaces. Let's find out a little more about them, shall we?

Chapter 3

The Family of Deities

The Minoan family of deities is large and colorful. Like their Bronze Age neighbors around the eastern Mediterranean, the Minoans were polytheists, celebrating a pantheon full of gods, goddesses, and deities who defy the gender binary. If you're acquainted with the Hellenic (Greek) pantheon, some of these names may sound familiar because the Greeks borrowed some of the Minoan deities and placed them into their own pantheon. Just bear in mind the Minoan faces of these deities may be very different from the Hellenic ones you already know about.

We don't know for certain how the Minoans organized their pantheon, but as with most cultures, it's likely the pantheon reflected the way their society was organized in terms of gender roles and family structure. In Ariadne's Tribe, we've pieced together fragments of myths and references to deities from Mycenaean and Hellenic Greek sources, taking into consideration that those are all from cultures that were very different from the Minoans, and some of them date to many centuries after Minoan culture ceased to exist. These collected pieces of myth gave us a basis from which to develop the pantheon further. But even with all that research, there were still a few blanks to fill in.

What we ended up doing is simply asking the deities themselves how they would like us, as modern Pagans, to relate to them. Our direct experience with the deities has led us to understand that the Minoan pantheon isn't easily organized into a tidy family tree like the Hellenic and Roman pantheons. Instead, it's more like a carnival fun house full of mirrors or, at the very least, an extremely complex and messy tapestry. Let me explain. But please don't panic; I'm going to mention a number of our deities here, and some of them may be unfamiliar. I promise, I'll describe each of them in detail further on in this chapter, including the pronunciations of their names. Please note that in order to avoid giving my publisher fits with the special characters, and because many people can't read IPA symbols, I've chosen not to use them for the pronunciations. Instead, I've done the best I can with English-language-style spelling.

The Minoan pantheon is a family headed by three mother goddesses, in much the same way the Minoans' matrilineal ancestors in Neolithic Anatolia probably organized their own human families, with mothers and grandmothers in leading roles. Rhea, Therasia, and Posidaeja are the three Great Mothers of our pantheon. They represent the sacred realms of Land, Sky, and Sea respectively. Each of the Great Mothers has two children, a Daughter and a Son, who are also connected to their mothers' realms:

Land: Rhea – Ariadne – Tauros Asterion
Sky: Therasia – Arachne – Korydallos
Sea: Posidaeja – Antheia – Dionysus

The Sons and Daughters are all psychopomps, soul-conductors for the dead who act as interfaces between humans and the Mothers, even though they're all very different from each other.

So far, the pantheon is pretty neat-and-tidy. But after this, the orderly pattern dissolves, and the family of deities gets messy. For instance, we have two other mother goddesses, Ourania and the Serpent Mother. Ourania is a cosmic goddess, the Great Cosmic Mother-of-All. In a sense, she's also Ariadne and Tauros Asterion's mother, and possibly also Antheia's, because each of them has starry or cosmic aspects. But she's also *everyone's* mother, because she is the cosmos itself. And the Serpent Mother has her own children, not a daughter-son pair but a triplicity, Thaena, Sydaili, and Eshuumna, who each have their own unique qualities.

This is just a small part of what I mean by the pantheon being a "carnival fun house full of mirrors." This issue is one aspect of an important saying we have in Ariadne's Tribe: *Individuation is problematic.*

As I mentioned in the chapter about the Minoan worldview, interconnection is a vital concept in Minoan spirituality. The deities are interwoven with each other in ways we don't fully understand. Some of them are twins or faces of each other, but they also function as separate deities in our spiritual practice. And they're also interwoven with us. There's a spark of the divine within not just every human being but every inspirited thing in the universe. Where's the line between us and them? That's a question we may never be able to fully answer, because there may not be a clean line at all.

The Minoan deities also don't fit neatly into pigeonholes. By that I mean, they don't seem to like hard labels. So we don't have a single goddess of luck and good fortune, for instance, and we have more than one deity who could reasonably qualify as a trickster. Minos is a moon god, but so are all the Horned Ones, even though Britomartis and Europa may originally have been sun goddesses.

Even the deities who do consent to labels insist on a certain amount of leeway. Rhea is the Grain Mother, sure, but Ariadne is the embodiment of the grain crop as it grows in the fields. And don't even get me started with the Serpent Mother. She's enigmatic, one and many, perhaps infinitely many. Then there are the deities who are only visible between two other deities: Thaena, Sydaili, and Eshuumna, who make up the Unseen Rainbow, with Eshuumna hidden between the other two. These three are Serpent deities, so the wiggliness makes sense, I suppose.

Let's look at how some of the other deities are related to each other. The Horned Ones are a good place to start. Again, don't panic; I'll share more details about all of them in their individual entries further on in this chapter. We have three pairs of deities associated with horned animals:

Cattle: The Minotaur and Europa
Goats: The Minocapros and Amalthea
Deer: The Minelathos and Britomartis

There's some evidence that Amalthea and Britomartis may be aspects of Rhea. When Rhea gives birth to the Divine Child in her cave at Midwinter, Amalthea nurses the infant Dionysus as if she, too, is the Divine Child's mother. One of Britomartis's names is Diktynna, connecting her with Mt. Dikte, Rhea's sacred mountain where her cave is located. But dance ethnology research suggests Europa was originally a sun goddess, connecting her with Therasia.

The three male Horned Ones appear to be reflections or faces of the three Sons. In Ariadne's Tribe, we consider the Minotaur to be a face of Tauros Asterion. You're probably familiar with the Minotaur from the Greek myth involving Ariadne and the Labyrinth. Our understanding of him is very different from the monstrous character in that myth. To us, the Minotaur is a beloved god, a friend and helper. And the Labyrinth isn't a dangerous maze, but a deeply moving pathway to spiritual growth, a single path that winds in to the center and then back out again. You can't get lost in it.

As we continue down the list of deities, we find that Daedalus and Talos are faces of Korydallos. Eileithyia is, among other things, the Underworld Sun Goddess, connected with Therasia. Zagreus is another face of Tauros Asterion. And Thumia and Kaulo are aspects of Therasia and Dionysus, respectively.

In addition to the complexity of their relationships with each other, many of the Minoan deities have multiple names. Deity epithets were common during the Bronze Age and for centuries afterward, not just in the Mediterranean but across Eurasia. So the Minoans weren't unusual in this regard. I've listed the epithets we use for each deity in their entry below.

Like I said, it's complicated. But it's also beautiful. The Minoan pantheon traces back to the Bronze Age and earlier. It's likely the family of deities was just as complicated back then, since Minoan religion layered the new on top of the old over the course of many centuries, much like the ancient Egyptians did.

The Minoans also had what we call *micropantheons*, or smaller cults that centered around individual deities or small groups of them and their stories. This type of religious practice continued past the LBA collapse and into the Iron Age around the eastern Mediterranean; it's very visible in classical-era Hellenic religion, for instance.

We've identified some of the Minoan micropantheons with the help of dance ethnology research. Each micropantheon focuses on a specific bit of mythos, like for instance the Mysteries (the Minoan version or precursor to the Eleusinian Mysteries) with Ariadne, Rhea, Iacchus, Eileithyia, and the Melissae. Many people in ancient Crete would have focused their spiritual practice on one or more micropantheons or specific deities rather than the pantheon as a whole. That's still a viable way to approach Minoan spirituality, if it appeals to you.

Since we're in relationship with these deities, they have connections not just with our ritual activities but also with our daily lives. This includes our occupations and hobbies as well as the raising of certain food crops. So each deity is the Benefactor of a certain type of human activity, which you'll find listed in their entries further along in this chapter. Each of the deities also has plants, animals, and other symbols associated with them. When you find these in Minoan art, you can be fairly certain the image is meant to refer to the deity the symbol belongs to.

There's a little more to "reading" Minoan art than just knowing which symbols belong to which deity. But it's not terribly complicated. Minoan art borrowed some iconography schemes from Mesopotamia, particularly the style of depicting a deity in between two of the same animal. Sometimes the deity is holding the animals, and sometimes they're just standing between them. When you see that kind of arrangement, which is common on Minoan seals, you know you're looking at a divine figure in the center. And the type of animal tells you *which* deity it is.

Another way deities are depicted in Minoan art is standing on top of a mountain, a city, or some other tall landscape. Both gods and goddesses are shown this way, most commonly on seals and seal impressions. Sometimes there's a detail in the image that tells us which deity is being depicted. For instance, there's a seal impression from Knossos called the Mountain Mother. It shows a female figure standing on top of a tall mountain. So this is a goddess. Flanking the mountain is a pair of lions, which tells us the specific goddess we're looking at is Rhea. There's another seal impression, from Chania, showing a male figure holding a staff and standing atop a big city. The staff identifies him as the god Korydallos. Once you know how to read the iconography, you start to see the deities emerging.

Sometimes, instead of a full human figure, you get a simplified, almost cartoonish tree, or even a column or pole between the two animals. This is a style of iconography that was popular around the eastern Mediterranean and across the Near East during the Bronze Age. In this case, the stylized tree or column always depicts a goddess and never a god. And as with the human images, the animals that flank the tree or column tell us which deity is being referenced.

Please note that a goddess shown flanked by a pair of animals is not necessarily Potnia Theron. This is a Greek term that means "Lady of the Animals." Homer first applied it to the Greek goddess Artemis, since she was connected with wild animals in her mythos. But over the past century or two, archaeologists and historians have sometimes used the term indiscriminately to refer to any goddess shown with animals, when they don't know any other way to identify which specific goddess they're looking at. That's not an accurate way to decipher Minoan sacred art. The type of animals shown along with the goddess are always a clue to her identity.

There's one more way to depict goddesses that's common in Minoan art: the lone seated female figure. Now, if you see a bunch of women seated together, like on the Grandstand fresco from Knossos, they're human. But if there's just one woman, the only seated person in the image, she's a goddess, or perhaps a human priestess embodying (being trance possessed by) a goddess. Sometimes there are other figures, male or female or both, in the scene with her. They're probably human. Some of them might be in worshiping poses like the Minoan salute, because, of course, that's what you do when you're in the presence of a deity. And sometimes there's an animal, like in the Goddess and Griffin fresco from Xeste 3 in Akrotiri. The fact that the female figure is seated tells us she's a goddess. The fact that she's flanked by a griffin tells us she is specifically the goddess Therasia.

What about all the other human-appearing figures in Minoan art? The vast majority of them are probably meant to depict ordinary mortals like us. Anyone performing the Minoan salute or any of its variants is a human worshiper, for instance. Other figures may be humans performing rituals. Sometimes we see tiny "floating figures" in the art. These are little human-shaped figures, both male and female, that hover near the heads of the people in the images. These are called epiphany figures, and archaeologists think they represent the appearance of the deity during the ritual, either to the group as a whole or perhaps via trance possession through one particular clergy person. So this is yet another way the deities appear in the art. It's a bit more subtle than being the centerpiece of the image, but it's more in keeping with what many of us experience in ritual. That was probably the case for the Minoans as well.

So let's get on with the details of the deities, shall we? In the listings below, I've put the Great Mothers (the Minoan Mother Goddesses) at the beginning out of respect for their position in the pantheon, in the order we usually list them in ritual based on their realms (land, sky, sea, the in-between spaces, the quantum foam). The rest of the family of deities follows in alphabetical order. The names of any other deities mentioned in a deity's listing will have their own entry elsewhere in this chapter.

The Great Mothers

Rhea (REE-ah or RAY-ah) is the Minoan mother goddess who presides over the sacred realm of Earth. We also call her Mountain Mother, Grain Mother, and Ida (ee-DAH). Just like many other ancient people, the Minoans considered the land where they lived to be divine and hence, sacred: a goddess. For the Minoans, this probably meant specifically the island of Crete. Like many of the Minoan deities, Rhea eventually ended up entangled in the classical Greek (Hellenic) pantheon. But she was originally from Crete. And like all the Minoan goddesses, in this pantheon she has no consort or husband. She stands independent and strong, mother to us all. She is the Earth Mother from whom our bodies are born and to whom they return at the end of our lives. And in between, she bestows great gifts upon us.

Rhea figures prominently in two major Minoan myth cycles, the birth of the divine child at Midwinter and the Minoan Mysteries, the precursor or early relative of the Eleusinian Mysteries. Let's look briefly at what those myths have to tell us. You'll find more details about both stories in the next chapter.

First, the Midwinter story. Recall, Ariadne is Rhea's daughter, and Tauros Asterion is her son. The fragments of Minoan myth that survived into classical times talk about Rhea giving birth to her divine son in her cave on her sacred mountain on Crete at the Winter Solstice. We think that originally, this tale involved Tauros Asterion. But by the end of Minoan times, Dionysus had taken that place in the story instead, which complicates his myth a bit, considering he's also Posidaeja's son. So we have Rhea, the Earth Mother, retreating to her sacred cave at sunset on Midwinter Eve, to give birth to the Divine Child Dionysus at sunrise on Winter Solstice morning. Astronomical alignments in the Throne Room of the Knossos temple complex suggest this sacred moment was celebrated there all the way to the end of Minoan times, even during the Mycenaean occupation.

The other myth that Rhea figures prominently in is the tale of the Minoan Mysteries. As a mother goddess, Rhea is the mother of all life on Crete: plant, animal, and human, including the grain crops. In the Minoan Mysteries, she descends to the Underworld at the end of the dead/dry summer season to remind her daughter Ariadne that it's time to return to the World Above for the growing season. Ariadne willingly spends the summer in the Underworld caring for the spirits of the dead. But because time passes differently there than it does in the World Above, she needs someone to come tell her when it's time to return for the growing season. Rhea's part in the story involves letting her beloved Daughter know the time has come. Since Ariadne goes to the World Below willingly to fulfill her role as Queen of the Dead, she doesn't need rescuing. But she does need her mother to let her know when it's time to move house, so to speak.

Besides mountains and caves, Rhea is also associated with the huge pottery jars the Minoans used to store oil, wine, and other staples for community feasting and distribution. They also sometimes buried their dead, especially infants, in these vessels, which are called pithoi (the singular is pithos). In other words, Rhea's pithos was the source of sustenance and the womb-symbol to which everyone returned after death. Given that one of Rhea's epithets is Pandora, which means "all-giver," it's quite possible the original story of Pandora involved not a stupid, silly girl letting all the evils out into the world. Instead, we think the original may have involved Rhea's pithos as a womb-symbol, much like the later bottomless cauldrons of European legend, the vessel from which everything flows and to which everything returns.

Rhea is the Benefactor of potters, since it's her body (clay/earth) that ceramic vessels like her mythical pithos are made from. As you might expect, she's also the Benefactor of farming, gardening, forestry and related occupations as well as environmentalism and ecology work.

She is associated with lilies, which in Minoan art are often stylized with an exaggerated double-curl that resembles breasts. Breasts figure prominently in Minoan sacred art, from priestesses with open-front clothing to animals suckling their young, to libation vessels shaped like animal teats. This is a reminder of the important position of the Mother Goddess in Minoan religion. The constant presence of breast imagery is also a reminder of the nurturing and nourishing aspects of motherhood, both human and divine.

Although Ariadne is the embodiment of the grain crop, Rhea is the Grain-Mother, the one who gives the gift of grain to humanity. Grain is sacred to her, as are the poppies that are still grown in the fields alongside wheat and barley around the Mediterranean.

The other plant associated with Rhea is the cypress tree. The ancient Greek writer Diodorus Siculus said there was a cypress grove dedicated to her at Knossos. So cypress trees belong to Rhea, and so does cypress wood, which can be offered to her in the form of incense. The type of this evergreen conifer that's native to Crete is *Cupressus sempervirens*, but whatever kind of cypress grows where you live will work just fine for offerings. I have a small grove of Leyland cypress (*Cupressus x leylandii*) that I've dedicated to Rhea.

Rock doves, a type of ground bird native to the Mediterranean, are Rhea's birds that show up repeatedly in Minoan frescoes and figurines. The lion is another of Rhea's animal associations. This one may trace back to Neolithic Anatolia, where the Minoans' ancestors were from and where we find lions in the sacred art connected with the Mother Goddess of that culture.

Therasia (teh-RAH-see-ah) is the sun goddess in the Minoan pantheon. You might have been expecting a sun god, but sun and sky gods were introduced into the Mediterranean by the Indo-Europeans. The Minoans, in contrast, were descended from a pre-Indo-European culture that maintained the Old European tradition of a sun goddess. In the Tribe, we also call her Kalliste ("the Beautiful"), Khelidon ("the Swallow"), the Sun-Mother, and Fire of Heaven. Of course, she presides over the realm of the sky. Fire and electricity also belong to her.

Dance ethnology research was key to finding Therasia, though we didn't discover her Minoan name. We don't know what the people of Bronze Age Crete called her, but she answers to the name Therasia now, and that's what's important for modern spiritual practice. Patricia Monaghan's excellent book *O Mother Sun!* also provided a lot of helpful comparative mythology information that helped us flesh out Therasia's mythos.

Over the course of the solar year, Therasia grows in power until she reaches her height at the Summer Solstice, when her heat and light beat down on Crete, creating the oppressive hot and dry "dead season" of the Mediterranean summer. Then her power wanes until, at the Winter Solstice, she retreats into her sacred cave to die and rebirth herself, like so many other Eurasian sun goddesses. Finally, at sunrise on Winter Solstice morning, the cycle begins again. It's possible the caves that are famous as Rhea's birthing caves were also originally Therasia's caves for her self-rebirthing. Or perhaps Therasia had her own sacred caves on Crete that have been lost to history. Both of these beloved mother goddesses retreat to a cave to give birth, in one way or another, at Midwinter. And Crete has many, many caves.

In addition to the sky and the sun, Therasia is also connected with volcanoes and hot springs, as are many other Eurasian sun goddesses. Hot springs exist in many volcanic areas. In fact, there are still hot springs around the eastern Mediterranean today, including in Greece, Turkey, and the Levant. Although there are no hot springs on Crete, it's likely there were some on Thera before the eruption in 1625 BCE. Ancient people thought of the sun as traveling beneath the earth at night, from the place where it sets in the west to the place where it rises again in the east. The idea (scientifically incorrect but mythologically interesting) is that, while the sun is beneath the earth at night, it heats up parts of the ground, creating volcanoes, as well as heating the subterranean waters, creating hot springs.

Therasia is the Benefactor of metalsmiths, especially those who work with bronze (the Minoans were a Bronze Age society) but including all metals, from iron to silver and gold. Though the ore for metalsmithing comes from the Earth, it's Therasia's gift of fire that allows us to transform it into attractive and useful metal objects.

Therasia is also associated with the date palm, a tree that dance ethnology research tells us is intimately connected with the pre-Indo-European sun goddess in the Mediterranean. So Therasia is also the Benefactor of the date crop and of those who grow date palm trees.

Her sacred bird is the swallow, a species that migrates south for the winter just as the sun shifts southward along the horizon as Winter Solstice approaches. The mythical creature the griffin is hers also, though it's probably an import from Mesopotamia and not originally Minoan. Griffins, with their lion bodies and eagle heads (and sometimes wings) appear repeatedly in Minoan art. You might be familiar with the griffins that flank the central seat in the Throne Room of the Knossos temple complex. Their presence suggests that whoever sat in that seat, a priestess perhaps, may have embodied Therasia in ritual.

Therasia's two sacred colors, red and gold, appear not just in Minoan art but also in two dye substances we associate with her: murex and saffron. The Minoans produced the rare murex dye centuries before it became famous as Phoenician purple, in several different locations on Crete and on the island of Chrysi just off the Cretan coastline. It takes thousands of murex sea snails to produce a single gram of dye, so it was a very labor-intensive process. The costly murex dye produces blood red to deep purple shades and was used in some Minoan frescoes where a purple pigment was needed, though sadly it has faded more than the other colors in the frescoes over the centuries.

The saffron crocus also produces a dye from the blood-red stigmas and styles of its lavender-tinted flowers. In a magical color transformation, the deep red saffron threads create a dye that's a rich, sunny yellow. Botanists think the Minoans are the ones who domesticated the saffron crocus back in the Bronze Age. The frescoes from building Xeste 3 in the Minoan city of Akrotiri show extensive fields of the plants, probably grown for both sacred and commercial purposes. So it's likely saffron was among the trade goods that built such wealth for the Minoans.

Posidaeja (poh-see-DYE-ah) is the Minoan goddess of the ocean and all the water on earth, both salt and fresh. We also call her Thalassa ("the sea"), Grandmother Ocean, and the Water-Mother. Her name is old enough that it appears on the Linear B tablets. Like all Minoan goddesses, she has no husband; Antheia and Dionysus are her daughter and son. She presides over the realm of the sea.

As an island culture, the Minoans were intimately familiar with the sea. They sailed all around the Mediterranean to trade and fished to provide food for their families. They lived their lives in Posidaeja's embrace. Food from the sea sustained them when land-based food sources weren't doing so well, like during droughts or after earthquakes. Sailing was one of the three major subcultures of Minoan Crete, along with farming and herding.

The sailing community had its own calendar based on the changing winds and tides, with a sailing season that began in late spring and ended in mid-autumn. These traditions of the sailing community's calendar survived into the Christian era on Crete, though many of the details were lost over time. The beginning and ending of the sailing season probably involved festivals that centered on Posidaeja's blessings and on offering gratitude to her for keeping their ships and boats safe on the water. The Minoans spent the winter repairing their ships and preparing for the next season's voyages, using storage spaces like the huge ship sheds (giant warehouses big enough to hold merchant ships) at Kommos on the south coast of Crete. If it weren't for all their ships and sailors, the Minoans wouldn't have been nearly so successful. It was those ships that brought in raw materials from all around the Mediterranean and transported Minoan finished goods to all their trading partners, helping to make them so wealthy.

Besides relying on the sea for the practicalities of food and trade, the Minoans were clearly fond of it as well. Sea creatures such as flying fish, squid, octopuses, coral, and tritons appear on Minoan ceramics and frescoes and as small faience models. The Minoans adorned their home and temple shrines with huge numbers of real seashells as well as hand-crafted artificial seashells made of faience, ceramic, and carved stone. The care they lavished on these aspects of their art suggests a deep and abiding affection for the sea. Sea creatures and other depictions of ocean life are Posidaeja's symbols; their presence in the art evokes her.

Although the Minoans were a Mediterranean people, Posidaeja is the goddess of all the oceans, or perhaps the one world ocean, if you look closely at how it actually works on a map. She is the Water-Mother, and this means all water, from the ocean to your local river, pond, lake, stream, or spring.

She is the Benefactor of sailors, boaters, and fishers, anyone who spends time in or on the water, especially if they make their living that way. Those activities are her domain. She and her sisters together are the Benefactors of ship-builders, with Rhea joining in for wooden boats and Therasia for metal ones.

The Serpent Mother is an enigmatic figure despite the fact that the Snake Goddess figurines from Knossos are such visible and iconic emblems of Minoan religion. Other epithets for this goddess are Basilissa and the Snake Goddess, but her real name is probably beyond human kenning. Her realm is the in-between spaces that are difficult to define, the places between the worlds and between the things in this world and the Underworld. Her place in the family tree of the Minoan deities is also slithery and equally hard to pin down, but we'll do our best. She exists beneath and beyond the material realm, but she can interact with us when necessary. Let's begin by examining her association with two practical aspects of life: grain and rain.

In the ancient Mediterranean, farmers considered snakes to be helpful allies because they ate the rodents that threatened the farmers' grain stores. The Minoans grew wheat, barley, and rye, relying on these staple foods not just for ordinary meals but for communal feasting at the temples and tombs. So everyone from ordinary households on up to the big temples valued snakes for their ability to protect the grain. This aspect of the Serpent Mother connects her with Rhea and Ariadne, the two goddesses who give the gift of grain to humanity and embody it during the growing season.

The Serpent Mother's connection with rain is quite an old one, going right back to Neolithic Anatolia, where the Minoans' ancestors came from. Containers decorated with "rain snakes" and perforated vessels used for rain-making rituals have been found at Neolithic sites in Anatolia and Old Europe. Similar perforated vessels have also been found at Minoan sites. Rain, after all, snakes its way through the sky and hisses as it hits the ground. This connects with grain in a way, because rainfall became even more important to humans when they gave up foraging and began to rely on agriculture to grow staple crops like wheat.

The Serpent Mother is an Underworld goddess; after all, snakes emerge from holes in the ground. And the true Labyrinth exists in the Underworld; the labyrinths that we draw and walk through in this world are material reflections of the real yet ineffable one. The Labyrinth is a place of healing and transformation, two things the Serpent Mother excels at. This includes both physical healing (that's her snake twining around Asclepius's rod, which you'll learn more about in his section below) and emotional/mental healing. Perhaps the ineffable Labyrinth is the Serpent Mother herself, drawing us through her being as we move from one lifetime to the next, safe within the winding pathways that always lead us home.

The Serpent Mother's slithery ways, so difficult for humans to understand, make her the Benefactor of translators and cryptographers, people whose work focuses on the transformation of communication from the incomprehensible to the understandable. We may never fully comprehend the Serpent Mother's way of being, but we can appreciate her presence in our lives.

Ourania (oh-RAH-nee-ah) is our Great Cosmic Mother whose realm is the whole cosmos. She is also called Starweaver or Mother-of-Darkness-and-Stars. She's the musician who plays the music of the spheres, but she's also the spheres themselves. If you view the universe as a single great consciousness, that would be Ourania. Her motions drive the cosmos, turning the wheels of time, so time as well as space is hers, that is, if they're even separate to begin with. If you're into quantum physics, you might think of her as the quantum foam. She's the substance out of which the entire universe is made, the conscious, sentient fabric of spacetime itself.

The stars are hers; astronomy, astrology, sacred calendars, and related pursuits are her domain. Astronomy was an important aspect of Minoan religion. We know this because the Minoan temples, tombs, peak sanctuaries, and other sacred buildings were built with alignments to sunrise and moonrise on specific dates as well as the heliacal risings of certain stars. The ordinary people may not have known much about astronomy beyond being able to name a few constellations. But the clergy must have spent many, many nights out on the temple rooftops, observing the stars, in order to develop their sacred calendars. To them, this process would have been holy.

Some people experience Ourania as an enormous black vulture, her wings spread out across the depths of space. Perhaps that's her we see on the pillars at Gobekli Tepe, a temple from the region and era the Minoans' ancestors came from. Some people also relate to Ourania as a cosmic cow goddess, with the spots on her hide as the stars that are spread out across the sky. Perhaps, eons ago, it was her milk that spurted to make the Milky Way. Interestingly, cattle and cowhide in Minoan art are almost always depicted as spotted. Whether Minoan cattle actually had spots, or whether the spots are symbolic, or perhaps both, we can't be sure.

As you might expect, Starweaver is the Benefactor of astronomers and astrophysicists as well as astronauts. Those who love the night sky and who study it as well as those who explore the cosmos are within her domain.

It can be easier to envision her as a force of nature or a cosmic power rather than an anthropomorphic goddess or even an animal. She can be a mysterious, shadowy figure. But she's also the beauty of the night sky. She reminds us that when we look up at the stars, we're also looking back in time, right back to the beginning of the universe, the beginning of her love for all existence.

The Family of Deities

Amalthea (ah-MAL-thee-ah) is a goat goddess, one of our Horned Ones. She's also called Adrasteia and Adamanthea. She is paired with the Minocapros, though they're not husband and wife the way many Hellenic and Roman deity pairs are. Like all the other Horned Ones, Amalthea is associated with the moon. She appears in myth as either a goat or a female figure, but not the half-human, half-goat form that is typical of the Minocapros.

Amalthea's most visible role in Minoan myth is as the wet-nurse for the Divine Child (Dionysus) who is born to Rhea in her cave at Midwinter. This may be where the Greeks got the story of her being Zeus's wet-nurse, since they called Dionysus "Cretan Zeus." Animals that give milk are prominent in Minoan art, often shown suckling their young. This is a reminder that the function of "mother" isn't restricted just to humans, and that the nurturing and nourishing aspects of mother goddesses come in many forms.

Amalthea is associated with both Mt. Dikte and Mt. Ida (now called Mt. Psiloritis), two mountains on Crete that contain caves that have been sacred to Rhea since Minoan times. It's Amalthea's connection with these two mountains and her position as Dionysus's wet-nurse that suggest she may be a twin or face of the goddess Rhea. In fact, some sources give Ida and Dikte as two of Amalthea's epithets. Whether or not she and Rhea are two facets of the same being, Amalthea is approachable as an individual deity with her own name and distinctive characteristics.

Ultimately, Amalthea is something of a wild goddess. Her epithet Adamanthea means "untamable goddess," suggesting an innate wildness to her. Although technically, goats are domesticated animals, on Crete they've straddled the divide between domestic and wild ever since they were brought to the island; goats go feral very easily, and there's still a large feral goat population on Crete. The local people call the feral goats *kri-kri* or *agrimi* and consider them to be distinct from the domesticated goats the people still keep in herds.

Amalthea is the source of an important symbol that persists in the modern world in both secular and sacred context: the cornucopia. It is, of course, one of Amalthea's horns, and from it flows an abundance of good things. This horn-shaped vessel is a variation of Rhea's pithos, the bottomless cauldron or jar that belonged to the old mother goddesses whose endless bounty provided for their people. This is yet another connection between the two goddesses.

This beloved goat goddess is the Benefactor of all the skills and occupations having to do with goat's milk, from ensuring your female goats produce plenty of milk to making cheese, yogurt, and butter. This includes hobby farmers and those who keep goats as pets as well as full-time farmers.

Antheia (an-THEE-ah or an-THAY-ah) is the goddess of beauty and love in all their great depth and profound significance. She's the Minoan face of Aphrodite, who is herself a pre-Greek goddess whose worship appears to have originated on the island of Cyprus then spread to Crete and the rest of the eastern Mediterranean. The Greek writer Hesychius said Antheia was the name used for Aphrodite at Knossos.

Antheia is Posidaeja's daughter but is also connected with Ourania, so she has both oceanic and starry aspects. Because of this "dual motherhood," she is also called the Star of the Sea and is associated with the Pleiades, the constellation whose heliacal rising in the spring marked the beginning of the sailing season in the ancient Mediterranean. As you might expect, she is also associated with the planet Venus; one of her symbols is the eight-petaled rosette that's common in Minoan, Levantine, and Mesopotamian art as a sign of this planet.

Antheia helps us find the beauty in the world: in ourselves, in each other, in nature, and even (or perhaps especially) in the activities of ordinary life. This is the kind of beauty that lives below the surface and is easy to overlook. She helps us realize that seeing this beauty is a way to connect with the divine, meeting it where it resides here with us in the material world, regardless of appearance. This quality within this goddess makes her the Benefactor of those who use creativity to express this underlying beauty and share it with others. This can take the form of any creative endeavor from music, writing, art, and storytelling to activities like dance, clothing design, home decoration, even flower arranging.

Because Antheia is Grandmother Ocean's daughter but is not herself a sea goddess, her domain is the seashore, the place where land and sea meet. Water birds are her animals: geese, ducks, and swans especially, but all kinds of shore birds including herons and cranes. They inhabit the liminal space between land and sea, the area that is Antheia's territory.

Her special flowers are the lily-like white sea daffodils (*Pancratium maritimum*), native wildflowers that grow along the dunes and beaches of Crete. Sadly, they're now endangered, so if you have the great good fortune to see any when you visit Crete, please don't pick them. White and yellow flowers in general are Antheia's symbols, especially the crown daisy (*Glebionis coronaria*) that's native to the Mediterranean. Myrtle (*Myrtus communis*) is also sacred to her. It's a native Mediterranean flowering shrub with delicate white flowers that turn into blue-black berries. The starry little five-pointed flowers are said to look like the planet Venus twinkling in the night sky.

Arachne (ah-RACK-nee) is a fate goddess who is also called Ananke ("necessity," as in the laws of nature), Web-Weaver, and Thread-Spinner. She's the sun goddess Therasia's daughter. Throughout Eurasia, sun goddesses have long been associated with fate, since we count our lives in days, from one sunrise to the next, one year to the next. The name Arachne comes from the pre-Greek word for "spider" from mainland Greece.

Many people know about Arachne from later Greek tales that paint her as a foolish mortal woman or even an actual spider. These stories give us a glimpse of a pre-Hellenic goddess who was so powerful, she couldn't be absorbed into the male-dominated Hellenic pantheon but instead had to be almost obliterated by being reduced to silly girl or a bug. But like her thread of fate, her story refused to disappear, and her name lives on today.

It's Arachne's thread that her sister Ariadne proffers in the Labyrinth-and-Minotaur legend, which dates to the classical Greek era, nearly a thousand years after the end of Minoan civilization. Most of the Minoan mythic fragments that survived into classical times ended up very garbled, hence the confusion between the two goddesses in this story. But thread as a symbol is a fate goddess property, so we can connect that important symbolic aspect of the Labyrinth tale with Arachne.

As a Minoan goddess, Arachne is different from other fate goddesses in that she's not the controlling designer of each person's individual destiny so much as she is the deity who tallies our life choices and keeps track of their outcomes. So she is, in a sense, the Counter of Consequences. It's her thread that we either climb to great heights or hang ourselves with. But the choices are always ours to make. This is a slightly different mindset than the concept of fate in most classical mythology. In Greek and Roman myth and literature, fate leans more toward predestination, a pre-written story that humans have no say in.

Arachne counts weaving and spinning tools as well as spiders and spiderwebs among her symbols. She's the Benefactor of all the fiber arts: spinning, weaving, basket making, sewing, quilting, embroidery, knitting, crochet, and so on. However, dyeing belongs to Potnia Chromaton, since colors are their own kind of magic. You can find her entry further down in this chapter. But in general, the fiber arts are Arachne's domain.

Ariadne (air-ee-ADD-nee or ahr-ee-AHD-nay) is Rhea's daughter and is also associated with Ourania. She is also called Lady of the Labyrinth and Queen of the Dead. She figures prominently in the Minoan Mysteries cycle of stories. Her role in the classical-era tale of the Labyrinth and the Minotaur also gives us a hint as to her earlier characteristics.

Ariadne's most well-known association is with the Labyrinth; the Linear B tablets refer to her as Potnia Labyrinthos: Lady of the Labyrinth. But the Labyrinth isn't a confusing maze at all. Instead, it's a unicursal (one route) maze that has one way in and the same way back out. In other words, you can't get lost. Labyrinths have been found all over the world dating back to very ancient times, so this is a concept that reaches far back into humanity's past.

The labyrinth is a spiritual tool that can be used to reach a person's own subconscious. Together with her brother Tauros Asterion in his form as the Minotaur, Ariadne guides us through the labyrinth into the cave of our own darkness, our own shadow self. There we can confront our inner demons and learn how to heal and become whole again. Our modern society can make it difficult to accept the parts of ourselves that aren't "goodness and light." But Ariadne understands that we're multi-faceted beings. It's the light that makes the shadow, and we must learn to accept both. Interestingly, the interplay of light and shadow was an important facet in Minoan ritual spaces. Many ritual areas had pier-and-door structures, whole walls made up of many doors side by side. These doors could be opened or closed in any combination to change the lighting, or lack thereof, in the room.

As I noted in the entry for the Serpent Mother above, the true Labyrinth is the path the soul takes to the Underworld upon death as well as the way back into this world upon reincarnation. It is also a pathway to healing and a way for spirit workers to access the Underworld. All material-world labyrinths are reflections of the true one and reminders of its existence. The concept of the Labyrinth as a path to and from the Underworld leads us to Ariadne's role in the Minoan Mysteries.

Ariadne is the embodiment of the grain crop, her mother's gift to humanity. The agricultural cycle is enshrined in the Minoan Mysteries. In this myth cycle, Ariadne descends to the Underworld freely (no abduction involved) to care for the spirits of the dead during the long, hot Mediterranean summer, which is the "dead time" in that climate. While she's there, she's accompanied by the goddess Eileithyia, who acts as her torch-bearer. Perhaps once, long ago, caring for the spirits of the dead was considered an honor and not a repulsive task that would only be performed under duress. Ariadne reminds us that our Beloved Dead are still beloved and still worthy of our attention and care.

While she's in the Underworld caring for the spirits of the dead, Ariadne is the Queen Bee, the head of the Melissae, the bee-spirit goddesses who are the guardians of the spirits of the dead. There's more about them further on in this chapter. The bee is an ancient symbol for the soul, and a buzzing sound like a hive of bees is a common experience among people who are entering shamanic trance to travel to the Underworld.

In the Underworld, Ariadne is the Queen of the Dead, queen not in the sense of ruling over them, but of caring for them as the family matriarch. In this role, she is also called Kala (KAH-lah). Our experience with Ariadne and her Queenly titles suggests that the concept of queen may originally have been a sacred one having nothing to do with ruling monarchy and everything to do with responsibility, care, and compassion for others.

Because time passes differently in the Underworld than in the World Above, Ariadne doesn't know when the summer is over. So as the rainy season is about to begin, Rhea descends to the Underworld along with Iacchus (the young Dionysus) as her torch-bearer. She tells her daughter it's time to return to the World Above.

As the rain softens the land so the farmers can plow the soil and plant their crops, Ariadne returns to the World Above with the first green sprouts in the fields, reminding us that life and death are not linear processes but part of a great recurring cycle. She remains "up here" with us throughout the growing season, rejoicing in the abundance of the grain crop. Then, at the springtime harvest, she dies along with the grain as it's cut down, returning to the Underworld to being the process all over again.

As the embodiment of the grain crop, Ariadne is the Benefactor of grain-growing. The Minoans had wheat, barley, and rye, but in the modern world we've expanded her responsibilities to include all the grains we now grow and use, regardless of where they originated.

In addition to grain, which points to Ariadne's World Above face, she is associated with three red things as symbols of her Underworld face: pomegranates, poppies, and red lilies. Red has long been the color of the dead and the World Below. Pomegranates, poppies, and lilies are native to the Mediterranean, and all three appear in Minoan art.

Asclepius (ah-SKLEP-ee-us), who is also called Paean (pye-AHN), is a healer god. In the Minoan pantheon, he's the son of the goddess Hygeia. This is backwards from their relationship in classical Greek myth. But in the Minoan pantheon, Hygeia is a face of the sun goddess Therasia, who along with the other Great Mothers presides over the rest of the pantheon, including all their sons. Asclepius is also connected with the Serpent Mother.

That's her snake coiled around his staff, usually called the Rod of Asclepius. Note that it's a single snake, which distinguishes it from Hermes's two-snake caduceus. The name Paean appears in the Linear B tablets.

As a healer, Asclepius's specialty is dreams, specifically a type of healing work called dream incubation. Many ancient cultures considered dreams to be the soul traveling to the Underworld, not in death, but only briefly during sleep. This is why dreams are so odd and also why they can give us insights into our waking lives. Ancestors, deities, and other spirit allies we can't hear so clearly when we're awake are able to share helpful information with us during dreams.

Dreams can be really weird, though, and it's not always easy to understand them. In the ancient world, dream incubation would have taken place in a temple, and there would have been trained clergy who were dedicated to Asclepius on hand when you woke up, to help you interpret your dreams. It's likely these clergy helped each person focus and meditate on their issue or question before falling asleep, in order to "tune" their dreams to the subject so their content would be more helpful. This practice is called directed dreaming.

Asclepius, like his mother Hygeia, is a Benefactor of people in the healing professions. This includes both conventional and alternative medicine. Dream incubation is Asclepius's primary domain, and in the modern world this also translates to healing modalities such as counseling and psychotherapy.

Britomartis (ancient Greek bree-TOE-mar-tees, modern Greek vree-TOE-mar-tees) is one of the Minoan Horned Ones. Her name, which isn't Greek and may originally have come from the Minoan language, means 'sweet maiden' or 'sweet virgin.' This is the type of epithet that was often used to pacify fierce or dangerous deities. She's a deer goddess, also called Diktynna, Lady of the Beasts, and the Huntress. She is paired with the

Minelathos. But like the other Minoan goddesses, she's not married to her male counterpart. And like all the Minoan Horned Ones, she has associations with the moon.

Deer are the wild animals among the Horned Ones, and Britomartis embodies that wildness. Her domain is the Cretan countryside, where herds of deer once roamed before modern hunters with rifles decimated their populations. She's the Huntress, an interesting juxtaposition considering one of her forms is a deer. Note that traditionally, only bucks are killed during hunting; does (female deer) are not. So the Minelathos is the Hunted while Britomartis is the One Who Hunts. Like the other female Horned Ones, Britomartis takes either human form or deer form but not the half-human, half-animal form that's common in depictions of, for instance, the Minotaur.

During later, post-Minoan times, Britomartis was shown on coins as Cretan Zeus's wet-nurse, just like Amalthea. We don't know whether this was part of her original set of attributes or whether it was added later to make her more like Amalthea. In our experiences with her, she has shown less of the mothering energies associated with Amalthea and Rhea and more of the wild young huntress energies we would expect from a goddess who is often compared with other huntresses like Artemis and Diana.

Britomartis has connections with Rhea via her epithet Diktynna, which evokes Rhea's sacred mountain, Mt. Dikte. In fact, Britomartis is associated with mountains in general, since they're wild, "uncivilized" territory. It's this wildness that lends her the epithet Potnia Theron (Mistress of the Animals or Lady of the Beasts). Although many Minoan goddesses are shown with animals, in most cases the animals in the art serve to identify the specific goddess; lions for Rhea, for example, or griffins for Therasia. This doesn't mean any of those goddesses are Potnia Theron. But in Britomartis's case, deer in particular evoke the wild animals of Crete, the ones the Minoans were never able to tame into livestock.

Britomartis's epithet Diktynna eventually led to her developing some new associations. Although the name refers to Mt. Dikte on Crete, by the time the classical Greeks came to know Britomartis, she was worshiped in several places around the eastern Mediterranean and not just on Crete. Apparently her original connection with Mt. Dikte was lost in the process of her transfer to those new locations, so people looked for another meaning for her name. Folk etymology having to do with the sea developed around the epithet Diktynna, with people thinking it might be connected with the Greek word for fishing nets (diktuon), even though it's not. So people decided she was also Lady of the Nets, although there's no evidence for her association with fishing or the sea before the classical era. Since we're focusing on her Minoan-era attributes here, we'll stick with her role as a deer goddess and a huntress. But in Hellenic Greece, she did have sea-based characteristics as well.

The Huntress is, of course, the Benefactor of hunters, specifically those who respect the wild animals and their lifeways and don't waste the bodies of the animals they hunt. Knowing when to choose not to hunt in order to safeguard the animal populations is also an important aspect of this process.

Daedalus (DEH-dah-lus or DEE-dah-lus) is the Minoan inventor and smith god. Invention, gadgetry, and tinkering are his domain. He's another face of the god Korydallos, who is Therasia's son, hence the connection with metal smithing. The god Talos is Korydallos's other face. All three names contain the *talos/dalos* segment we think may have been this deity's original name.

You're probably familiar with some stories about Daedalus, his building the Labyrinth to hide the supposedly monstrous Minotaur and his escape from Crete with his son Icarus using hand-crafted wings. But these tales come from the Roman writer Ovid, who lived nearly 1500 years after the destruction of the

Minoan cities. Ovid created his stories from garbled fragments that survived from Minoan times combined with his own imagination, so they may not be at all accurate to the originals.

In *The Iliad*, Homer relates that Daedalus built Ariadne's dancing floor. It's thought the circular folk dances of Crete originated at harvest festivals where dancing took place on the outdoor threshing floors. This may be how Daedalus came to be associated with the Labyrinth, which later people thought was a complex building but which may originally have been a design marked on floors for rituals or sacred dances.

Daedalus is the skilled craftsman who helped people learn to use many of the gifts the Great Mothers gave to humanity. So he is the Benefactor of all the skilled crafts and trades that use the hands but that aren't already in the domain of other deities. The fiber arts belong to Arachne and pottery to Rhea, and Daedalus shares with Therasia the position of Benefactor of metal smiths. So think of him in terms of hobby or professional wood working and carving, mechanics (everything from repairing automobiles to watchmaking), and any kind of gadget-making, with a nod to Therasia for gadgets that involve electricity.

The Daktyls (DAK-tills) **and Hekaterides** (heh-kah-TEH-ree-days) are the Hands of Great Skill, demigods and demigoddesses who represent the magic inherent in two specific types of handcrafts: metal smithing and pottery production. These demideities have connections with Rhea, Therasia, and Daedalus.

The Daktyls and Hekaterides are Rhea's creations. They were born out of the Earth where the Great Mother dug her fingers when she was in labor in her sacred cave on Midwinter night before giving birth to the Divine Child at sunrise the next morning. The five Daktyls arose from the marks her right hand made in the Earth, and the Hekaterides arose from the marks made by her left hand.

The Daktyls are demigods, and the Hekaterides are demigoddesses. The Daktyls have as their domain metal smithing, while the Hekaterides are associated with pottery. Both of these crafts involve taking the substance of the earth, the Mountain Mother Rhea, and transforming it with Therasia's sacred gift of fire and the skill of human hands. Metal smithing begins with metal ore from the earth, and pottery begins with clay. These demideities support any human of any gender who practices either of these skilled crafts, professionally or as a hobby.

Dionysus (dye-oh-NYE-sus) is also called the Undiluted One, the Liberator, and Iacchus, and is probably a familiar deity to you. He's one of the most multi-layered gods in the classical-era Hellenic pantheon, a syncretization of the Minoan deity with a similar Phrygian ecstatic god called Sabazios. But for our purposes here, we're taking him back to his Minoan roots. His name appears in the Linear B tablets in the form *di-wo-nu-so*, suggesting he was originally called something closer to Divonusos. In the Minoan pantheon, he's Posidaeja's son. And he's the god of the vine, the solar year, and sacred intoxication.

Dionysus is so much more than a party god, which is the way much of the general public views him. As Posidaeja's son, he's connected with dolphins and is the psychopomp for sailors who die at sea. There's a whole set of myths that connect him with the sea and sailing, though they're not as well-known as some of his other stories. His role as a psychopomp is underscored by the fact that many ancient cultures considered the sea to be a gateway to the Underworld. It's likely not a coincidence that Homer called the Aegean the *wine-dark sea*. The sea was incredibly important to the Minoans; it was the basis of their economy and the source of a major portion of their food supply. Dionysus was a part of their seagoing lives as well as their land-based activities.

On land, Dionysus was first and foremost the god of the vine, of the grape harvest and winemaking and the ecstasy that comes from alcoholic beverages. We celebrate Dionysus and the grape harvest at the Feast of Grapes. At this time, Dionysus dies as the grapes are cut from the vine. Then he travels to the Underworld, something he can do easily because he's a psychopomp. Part of his gift to the people is wine and other fermented beverages, which can take us out of our ordinary mindset and into altered states of consciousness. He also gives us the grape harvest in general: fresh grapes, grape juice, and raisins, all of which would have been important foods in the Minoan kitchen. Some people think Dionysus began as a fungal god, with entheogenic mushrooms as his original attribute, and later shifted to the fungal fermentation that allows us to brew wine, mead, and beer.

One of the interesting aspects of Minoan religion is that it evolved over the centuries, adding new layers as the culture shifted and changed. Much like the Egyptians, the Minoans appear to have simply added new festivals, rituals, and even deities to their religion over time, layering them on top of what was already there instead of replacing the old with the new. Foreign influence from the Mycenaeans was also prominent in the last few centuries of Minoan civilization, especially during the era when the Mycenaeans occupied Knossos. While a number of aspects of Minoan religion changed over time, Dionysus appears to have experienced more shifts than most of the other deities, possibly because he was so popular with the Mycenaeans.

Although it's likely Rhea's son Tauros Asterion was the original Divine Child born in her sacred cave at Winter Solstice, Dionysus eventually took on that role. When this happened, he became more than just the God of the Vine; he also became a year-king, his birth at Winter Solstice marking the turning point in the solar year. So he had two cycles, the growth and harvest of the grapes in the vineyards and the birth of the Divine Child at Midwinter.

The Mycenaeans loved Dionysus so much, they thought he belonged at the top of the Minoan pantheon, in keeping with their cultural values of men being dominant over women, therefore gods being dominant over goddesses. So they called him Cretan Zeus, equating him with the head of their own pantheon. Over the centuries, this was shortened to just Zeus, which is how we've ended up with stories of "Zeus" being born to Rhea in her cave on Crete. These stories refer not to the Hellenic Olympian deity, but to the Minoan Dionysus.

As befits the God of Vine and Wine, Dionysus is the Benefactor of grapes and grape-growing, fungal fermentation of all kinds, and wine-making in particular, but also mead-making and beer brewing. Although many of our deities are connected with various kinds of ecstatic and trance activities, Dionysus is the main Benefactor specifically for ecstatic dance.

Eileithyia (ancient Greek ay-LAY-thee-ah, modern Greek ee-LEE-thee-ah) is the Minoan midwife-goddess. Her name is pre-Greek, so when we call to Eileithyia, we may be using a form that's very close to her original Minoan name. She presides over the transitions of birth and death, including protecting humans during pregnancy, labor, and childbirth. Along with the Melissae, she assists the soul's journey into the body at birth and out of it at death. These liminal times are her specialty. As a divine midwife, she can also support us in rebirthing ourselves into new relationships and new phases of life.

Her sacred cave on Crete, near the north central coast of the island, was first used in Neolithic times, somewhere between 7000 and 5000 BCE. It continued to be a site of sacred pilgrimage all the way into the Christian era, which makes sense, given that pregnancy and childbirth are such potent and dangerous times, especially in the era before modern medicine. We've already seen sacred caves in conjunction with two of our mother goddesses, Rhea and Therasia, as well as the goddess Britomartis. Cave shrines were an important focus of Minoan religion and a strong symbol of the power of Minoan goddesses.

Eileithyia is also connected with the Eleusinian Mysteries, which appear to have had an early or precursor version on Crete. The name of the Greek town where the Mysteries were held, Eleusis, isn't Greek. Instead, it appears to be associated with both Elysium (the abode of the ancestors) and Eileithyia's name, which as I mentioned above is pre-Greek.

One of Eileithyia's attributes is a flaming torch, which the later Greeks said stood for the burning pain of childbirth. I'd like to suggest an alternate interpretation. If the torch is one of her symbols from an earlier time when women were more honored and cherished, then it might be a symbol of comfort for the laboring mother, a light in the darkness and a focal point during the travails of labor. It might also represent the passage of the baby from the darkness of the womb to the light of the world.

There's another possible meaning to Eileithyia's torch as well. In the Minoan Mysteries, Eileithyia is Ariadne's torch-bearer in the Underworld during the summertime "dead season" when the Queen of the Dead cares for the spirits there. This suggests Eileithyia is, therefore, the Underworld or Dark Sun Goddess, and we consider her to be a face of our sun goddess Therasia.

The midwife goddess is, of course, the Benefactor of human midwives, both those who welcome newborn babies into this world and those who help the dying make their transition to the Otherworld. Both of these are sacred callings that deserve far more recognition and respect than they are often given these days.

Europa (yoo-ROE-pah), who is also called Pasiphae or the Moon-Cow, is a cow goddess. She's paired with the Minotaur.

Like the other Minoan goddesses, she isn't married to her male counterpart. There's some evidence, via Mediterranean folklore and dance ethnology, that Europa and her double/twin Pasiphaë were originally solar goddesses, similar to the Egyptian solar cow-goddess Hathor. But by the Bronze Age, her lunar aspect had become more important, and she is now associated with the moon, just like the other Horned Ones. In the mythos, Europa always appears as either a cow or a human and never the half-human, half-cattle kind of appearance that's so often associated with the Minotaur.

It's possible Europa was originally a Levantine goddess, since Hellenic myth describes her as coming from Phoenicia. Her twin Pasiphae is described as having come from the shore of the Black Sea, specifically the city of Colchis which is located in the modern country of Georgia. So like Antheia, this goddess may have traveled to Crete from elsewhere. Or she may simply be the Minoan face of a much older goddess who began in Anatolia, among the people who migrated not just to Crete but to the Levant and other places during the Neolithic era. If that's the case, she may have had different names in different places around the eastern Mediterranean, with her Minoan name lost to time.

In addition to extensive human breast imagery, Minoan art includes depictions of long-horned cows suckling their calves, cow-headed rhytons (offering pitchers), and rhytons shaped like animal teats. These are a reminder that nurturing and nourishing are among the maternal characteristics the Minoans revered in their goddesses, even in non-human form.

Besides bovine imagery such as cows, udders, and horns, Europa is also associated with spring-blooming crocuses. These flowers are not the same as the saffron crocus, which blooms in the autumn and whose dried stigmas and styles make the famous spice. Spring-blooming crocuses appear in the fragments of myth about Europa that survived into classical times. Europa is the Benefactor of bovine dairying and all associated occupations having to do with cow's milk, including cheese-making and the production of other dairy products like yogurt and butter.

Hygeia (hye-JEE-ah) is the goddess of healing and good health. In later Hellenic myth, she is Asclepius's daughter. But in the Minoan pantheon, she's a face of the sun goddess Therasia, and Asclepius is her son. She's also connected with the Serpent Mother, since snakes are Hygeia's symbol as well as Asclepius's. The name Hygeia is simply the ancient Greek word for health. We don't know what the Minoans called her.

While Hygeia can be called on to aid in healing from a variety of mental and physical illnesses, her greatest strength is helping a person achieve and maintain robust good health for the long term. She's the one to call on when you're run down or fighting chronic illness, or in the case of children who are failing to thrive. Of course, you should also seek appropriate medical care. The deities can help us, but we must also do our utmost to help ourselves and each other in the material sphere. Hygeia is especially good at helping people set boundaries in order to safeguard their own health and well-being and that of the people they're caregivers for, such as children and the elderly.

As you might expect, she's the Benefactor of people in the healing professions, both conventional and alternative medicine. Herbalism figures prominently in Hygeia's domain, so herbalists are particularly under her benefaction. But all healing modalities, particularly those dealing with physical health, are her domain.

Kalaeja (kah-LYE-ah) is the goddess associated with the Tribe ritual of Confluence, which I'll explain further down, in the chapter about ritual. Kalaeja is all about movement, flow, and combining yourself with others and with your environment.

We connected with her via shared gnosis while we were developing the rite of Confluence. The lesson she teaches is that everything and everyone you connect with changes you, and you can never go back to being the same again. We're all alive in Kalaeja's dance, flowing together with her and with each other. We are the dancers and she is the dance, and vice versa. We don't usually call on her outside the confines of the Confluence ritual, but she's present in every aspect of life in which we reach the flow state and become one with whatever we're doing.

Kaulo (COW-loh, with the first syllable pronounced like the English word *cow*) is a god of physical pleasure and joy. He's paired with Thumia, but like the other Minoan male-female deity pairs, they're not husband and wife. He is a face of the god Dionysus.

Kaulo helps us find sacred joy in the pleasurable physical activities of life, from dancing to cuddles, hugs, massages, and sex. Any kind of joyous, consenting physical activity falls under his purview; not just sex, but all kinds of physical expression and connection. Kaulo enjoys humor, especially bawdy humor, as long as it doesn't punch down; he likes to remind us that laughter is sacred and that we shouldn't take ourselves too seriously. He can help us experience joy then hold it in our hearts as we move through life.

Although we refer to Kaulo as a god, he's a bit genderfluid. Neither he nor Thumia fits easily into any kind of binary human category, even though we call them "god" and "goddess" for simplicity's sake. Of course, human gender doesn't really apply to the deities, but we use it as a descriptor to help us understand them and connect with them. In addition, if you think of Thumia and Kaulo as standing next to each other, you can imagine a third deity, called ThumiaKaulo, standing between them, a blend of the two who is both masculine and feminine at the same time. The Two imply the existence of the Third, magically speaking.

Kaulo is associated with the color red, especially red sashes and belts, as well as any kind of small, jingling bells, like the hip and ankle bells often worn by belly dancers. He's the Benefactor of all occupations that involve the joyful or pleasurable use of the body as the primary focus, from dancers to massage therapists to sex workers, with a special emphasis on male-presenting sex workers.

Korydallos (koh-ree-dah-LOS) is Therasia's son. He is also called the Red Champion, the Dancer, and the Lark (his name Korydallos is the Greek word for "lark," the bird). Dance ethnology shows us that the Red Champion still exists in folk dances around the Mediterranean today.

Korydallos is an exuberant, playful figure, not quite a trickster, but close. He laughs and dances and loves word play like jokes and puns, as long as they never punch down. He reminds us not to take ourselves too seriously. You might think of him as sparkling and shining, perhaps singing and laughing jubilantly and helping us find the joy in life.

He carries a staff as his spirit tool as he travels between the worlds. This staff can generate lightning; recall that Korydallos is Therasia's son, and electricity belongs to her. We also associate bronze daggers with him, especially the fancy kind that young Minoan men wore upright at the waist right next to their codpiece. Interestingly, Cretan traditional dress for men still includes a dagger worn in much the same way (no codpiece, though).

Because his mother is Therasia, Korydallos is associated with bronze. Although modern people may think of bronze as dark brown in color because that's what the aged bronze artifacts in museums tend to look like, brand new bronze is actually a bright golden color. This gold, along with the red of red ochre, are his colors.

His connection with bronze and metal smithing reminds us that Korydallos has two other faces: Daedalus and Talos. You can find out more about them in their entries elsewhere in this chapter. All three names contain the *talos/dalos* segment that we think may have been this deity's original name.

Because of his fondness for wordplay and jokes, Korydallos is the Benefactor of humor in all its many forms. So if you're a standup comedian, a comic artist, or a writer of humor, he's your Benefactor for those activities. He's also the Benefactor of word play of all sorts, including poetry, puns, and riddles, particularly when the wordplay helps us understand ourselves and the world around us more deeply.

The Melissae (MAY-lih-say, MAY-lih-sye) are bee-spirit goddesses who are guardians of the spirits of the dead. Their name comes from the words for honey (meli) and honeybee (melissa) that were borrowed into Greek from some pre-Greek language, possibly Minoan. We also call them the Golden Ones and the Buzzing Ones.

The Melissae are connected with several other deities, including Amalthea. When Dionysus was born to Rhea in her sacred cave, Amalthea nursed the baby, and the Melissae fed him honey. So Crete was the land of milk and honey!

We also associate the Melissae with Ariadne, who is the Queen Bee, the head of the Melissae, when she's in the Underworld caring for the spirits of the dead. The Melissae assist Ariadne in her role as guardian of the dead during the Mediterranean summer when she's in the World Below. So the Melissae participate in the Underworld part of the cycle of the Minoan Mysteries.

Eileithyia also has a connection with the Melissae, since she delivers the soul of the newborn baby along with its body as it's born into the World Above. The souls she delivers have been cared for by the Melissae until their time to be born and are assisted into their new lives by the bee-spirit goddesses.

53

The buzzing of the Melissae is a sign of trance induction for many spirit workers, who hear a sound like a hive of buzzing bees as they enter altered states of consciousness. Perhaps Minoan spirit workers felt they were hearing the Melissae themselves, greeting them as they journeyed to the Underworld.

In the Bronze Age, sweet foods were far rarer than they are now, and honey was a prized substance, used not only for human consumption and for medicine but also as offerings for the spirits of the dead, to wish them a sweet afterlife. The Minoans were renowned beekeepers, producing honey they used to sweeten food and beverages and to brew mead. So these lovely bee-spirit goddesses are the Benefactors of beehives and beekeeping, an occupation associated with the Beloved Dead since ancient times.

The Minelathos (mih-nee-LAH-thos) or Moon-Stag is one of the male Horned Ones. He's an antlered deer god, paired with Britomartis but not married to her. Like the other male Horned Ones, he's associated with the moon and was probably represented by sacrificial animals in the practice of Minoan religion. And as with the other male Horned Ones, we don't know what his Minoan-era name was. In the case of the Minelathos, we call him the name Victorian-era mythologists coined to be similar to the name of the Minotaur but to reference deer rather than bulls.

The Minelathos and Britomartis are a little different from the other pairs of Horned Ones in a couple of ways. As far as we know, deer were never a domesticated livestock animal on Crete. Instead, they were hunted; there's archaeological evidence the Minoans ate venison. So although deer were included alongside cattle and goats as food animals in Bronze Age Crete, they were never under human control. The domain of the Minelathos is the same as that of the deer on ancient Crete: the woods and meadows of the countryside, away from the cities and towns.

Since deer were hunted instead of raised domestically, hunting figures in the Minelathos's characteristics. He's the Hunted One, while Britomartis is the Huntress. In other words, the Minelathos is the sacrifice. This puts him in the category of dying-and-reborn gods, whose ability to symbolically die and descend to the Underworld gives them the ability to intercede on our behalf in that realm. So he's a shamanic god.

Considering that Britomartis is specifically connected with the Minelathos's demise, it's likely Minoan deer sacrifices were performed by priestesses. Minoan art depicts both women and men wearing the animal-hide skirts associated with animal sacrifice. As was usually the case in the ancient world, sacrificial animals would have been used for food after the ritual. Wasting meat would have been considered disrespectful to the animal and the deity it represented.

We don't know whether the Minelathos represents a particular species of deer or just deer in general. The Minoans hunted and ate roe deer; the bones are in evidence at archaeological sites. And fallow deer appear in Minoan art. So it's probable both kinds of deer lived on Crete during the Bronze Age. Sadly, there are no deer left on Crete today. When firearms were introduced to the island, over-enthusiastic hunters killed them all.

As with the other two male Horned Ones, we have artwork from Minoan seals showing the Minelathos as a half-human, half-animal figure, in this case half-stag. Dance ethnology research suggests this appearance may have been associated with trance practices involving shape-shifting. This makes sense, given the god's shamanic characteristics.

The Minelathos is another face of the god Dionysus, and as such, he is also called Divono, a simplified version of Dionysus's name as recorded in the Linear B tablets.

The deer is the wild animal among the Horned Ones, so the Minelathos is the Benefactor of those who study and protect wildlife, whether that's as biologists or park rangers or activists.

General environmentalism is Rhea's territory, but wildlife in specific is the Minelathos's benefaction.

The Minocapros (mee-noe-CAP-ros) or Moon-Goat is the goat-god of the Horned Ones. He's paired with Amalthea but isn't married to her. Like the other male Horned Ones, he's associated with the moon and was probably represented by sacrificial animals in the practice of Minoan religion. And as with the other male Horned Ones, we don't know what his Minoan-era name was. In the case of the Minocapros, we call him the name Victorian-era mythologists coined to be similar to the name of the Minotaur but to reference goats rather than bulls.

In addition to cattle, goats abound in Minoan art. While the Minelathos represents wild animals and the Minotaur represents domesticated ones, the Minocapros straddles the divide. In ancient Crete, just like today, there were both domesticated and feral goats. Their domain is the hills and mountains that run like a giant spine down the center of the island. There's still a goat-herding subculture in the mountains of Crete today. The people of ancient Crete relied on domesticated goats for meat, milk, and hides, just as they did cattle.

As with the other two male Horned Ones, artwork on Minoan seals shows the Minocapros as a half-human, half-animal figure, in this case half-goat. Dance ethnology research suggests this appearance may have been associated with trance practices involving shape-shifting. This makes sense, given the god's shamanic characteristics. He is, of course, a sacrificial dying-and-reborn god. The literal death of the animal would have represented the symbolic death of the god as he traveled to the World Below.

In the modern Minoan pantheon, the Minocapros is one of Korydallos's faces. One of the names we call him is Vikaro (VEE-kah-roh), a name we discovered through shared gnosis and research into the story of Icarus and the goat-herding culture of western Crete. The Minocapros is the Benefactor of goat-herding and goats in general, whether on a large farm or a small homestead, or as pets.

Minos (MEE-nos or MYE-nos), the famous character after whom Sir Arthur Evans named Minoan civilization, is not a king but a god. Minos is a wise moon god whose main residence is in the Underworld. We don't know for certain what Minos's name means, but it may be a reference to the moon. It appears in Homer's works, though, so it's old enough, it's probably the name the Minoans used for him, or very close to it. We associate him with the moon, the stars of the Underworld, silver mirrors, and still water that reflects the night sky.

Minos's story appears in several different versions in classical literature, but there are two parts that are consistent across all the stories: He periodically died and descended to the Underworld, and he was a lawgiver and a judge of the dead. These two parts are interconnected, since he judges the dead when he's in the Underworld. And it's from the Underworld, or perhaps from the deities there such as the Great Mothers, that he receives the laws. Several versions of his story talk about him descending to Rhea's cave (caves being gateways to the Underworld) and receiving the laws from the goddess there.

Although the later Greek legends say Minos's laws were the ones the Greek government was based on, that's not really likely. Minoan culture was substantially different from Hellenic culture, and the two were separated by many centuries. It's also unlikely that any significant amount of administrative knowledge survived the destruction of the Minoan cities and the Late Bronze Age collapse. What's more likely, as some versions of the story suggest, is that the laws were the ones Minos used to judge the spirits of the dead. Perhaps he doesn't judge the dead in a "going to heaven or hell" sense, but instead helps them review their lives and learn from their experiences. He takes part in the Underworld phase of the Minoan Mysteries, along with Ariadne.

The stories say Minos returns to the Underworld every ninth year, which suggests the ancient practice of *inclusive counting*. This was a common counting style in the ancient world but one that's unfamiliar to many people today. The reason it's unfamiliar is that we begin our counting with zero, a concept most ancient cultures didn't have. In other words, "every ninth year" means Minos returned to the Underworld at the end of eight years. This connects him to the sacred calendar in another way.

The Minoans were accomplished astronomers, keeping track of the movements of a variety of celestial objects. We know this from artifacts and from astronomical alignments in Minoan buildings. One set of cycles they followed was the octaeteris, a sacred calendar that's eight solar years long. Eight solar years happen to match up to five Venus cycles and 99 moon cycles. In Ariadne's Tribe, we call this eight-year-long cycle the Minos Year.

Although we call the whole cycle the Minos Year, Minos is specifically connected with the moon. The possible meaning of his name suggests it, as does the number 14 (the seven Athenian youths and seven maids who were shipped off to Crete to be Minotaur chow every year in the Greek version of the story). The number 14 was consistently linked with the moon in the ancient world because 14 days make up half a lunar cycle.

Minos is a triple god. This aspect of him shows up in Homer's tales, where he's always described as being one of three brothers. The other two names vary from one version of the story to another, but Minos is always the eldest and highest-ranked of the three. In the Tribe, his three faces are connected with the three Sons: Tauros Asterion, Korydallos, and Dionysus. Minos is the elder, Underworld reflection of them, and he has three faces that correspond with the Sons.

The names we use for his three faces in the modern Minoan pantheon may look familiar, but don't prejudge them. We came to them via comparative mythology with a large dose of shared gnosis. In the context of Minoan spirituality, they're a good bit different from the personalities of the deities who carry these same names in classical Greece, many centuries after the Minoans were long gone. The name we use for the face of Minos associated with Tauros Asterion is Aides (EYE-days). The one for the face of Minos associated with Korydallos is Ares (AH-rays). And the one for the face of Minos associated with Dionysus is Aulos (OWL-ohs).

Minos, this Underworld god who is wise and insightful, is the Benefactor of divination and diviners, both amateur and professional. This includes all divination methods, regardless of their connection (or lack thereof) with the Minoan world.

The Minotaur (MIH-noh-tor or MYE-noh-tor). This much-maligned being is not a monster but a beloved bull-god, one of the Horned Ones, whose female counterpart is Europa. Of course, as you've probably figured out by now, they're not a married pair, but simply two faces of the bovine Horned Ones. The Minotaur is a face of Tauros Asterion. In the Tribe, we sometimes call him Lugoso (LOO-goh-soh), a name we discovered via shared gnosis.

Like the other male Horned Ones, he's associated with the moon and was probably represented by sacrificial animals in the practice of Minoan religion. We don't know what his Minoan-era name was. The earliest references to him in Greek literature date to the third century BCE, nearly a thousand years after the last Minoan city fell. At that point, he's called the Minotauros, a name that appears to be a combination of the name of the god Minos plus "tauros," the Greek word for bull.

As with the other two male Horned Ones, artwork on Minoan seals shows the Minotaur as a half-human, half-animal figure, with the animal half being a bull. Dance ethnology research suggests this appearance may have been associated with trance practices involving shape-shifting. This makes sense, given the god's shamanic characteristics.

His most important responsibility is as the guardian of the Labyrinth. In this role, he collaborates with Ariadne to guide us through that winding path and help us face the shadows we find at the center, our own fears and insecurities. He does what all shamanic gods do when they travel between the worlds: He helps us find renewal, leave behind the stuff that no longer serves us, and be reborn in our own lives or into the next life.

Our beloved Minotaur is the Benefactor of cattle husbandry, with an emphasis on respect for the animals and their quality of life.

Potnia Chromaton (POTE-nee-ah kroh-MAH-ton), literally "Lady of the Colors," is a face of the weaver-fate goddess Arachne, with close ties to Arachne's mother Therasia. While the textile arts in general (weaving, spinning, sewing, and so on) are Arachne's domain, Potnia Chromaton is the goddess to whom the colors belong. Dyeing, painting (analog and digital), and other activities whose main focus is color are her domain. In this case, "painting" includes both making colorful pictures and painting the walls in your house or even the outside of a house or other building. If color is involved, it's Potnia Chromaton's domain.

There's a sense in which color is magic, because it's not a solid thing but rather, a reflection of certain wavelengths of light. Light comes from Therasia and is its own kind of magic. Potnia Chromaton is the Benefactor of those who work with color: dyers, painters, photographers, filmmakers, and so on.

Talos (TAH-los) is a face of the god Korydallos, closely associated with Korydallos's other aspect, the inventor-smith god Daedalus. All three names contain the *talos/dalos* segment that we think may have been this deity's original name. Their mother Therasia gave the gift of metal smithing to humanity, hence their connection with it. The word talôs can mean "the sun" in the Cretan dialect of Greek, and Talos was associated with the sun in classical-era mythology. This reinforces the connection with Korydallos, who is the son of the Sun Goddess.

In the Greek version of the story, Talos was a mythical bronze automaton who guarded the shores of ancient Crete. In other words, he was the embodiment of the tradition of bronze smithing and the ingeniousness of the smiths, inventors, and other craftspeople of ancient Crete who worked with bronze, copper, and precious metals.

The Greek mythographer Pseudo-Apollodorus said Talos was the last of the "bronze generation" and was a "bronze man." Perhaps he wasn't a mechanical bronze man but rather, a patron deity of bronze-smithing in the era before that skill died out and was replaced by iron-working. Talos is the Benefactor of bronze smiths and others who work with that metal.

Tauros Asterion (TOH-rohs ah-STAY-ree-on), the Starry Bull, is the son of the Earth Goddess Rhea. The Minotaur and Zagreus are two of his faces. His name gives us a clue to the two main aspects of his character; Tauros means "bull" and Asterion means "starry one."

While we take the first part of his name, Tauros, from his association with cattle, his second name, Asterion, comes from three references in classical literature. The first two are from Pseudo-Apollodorus, the pen name of a Greek or Roman author who lived in the first or second century BCE, and Diodorus Siculus, a Greek historian who lived in the first century BCE. These men were writing about 1400 years after the destruction of the Minoan cities, recording garbled fragments of Minoan myth that had survived the centuries via a combination of oral and written sources.

Here's what they had to say about Asterion:

A son of Teutamus, and king of the Cretans, who married Europa after she had been carried to Crete by Zeus. He also brought up the three sons, Minos, Sarpedon, and Rhadamanthys, whom she had by the father of the gods. (Apollod. iii. 1. § 2, &c.; Diod. iv. 60.)

Teutamus was a 4th century BCE Macedonian military commander, so he was added to the story at a very late date, when the Minoans were long gone. Europa is a Minoan Horned One who was borrowed into the Hellenic pantheon. And Minos, Sarpedon, and Rhadamanthys are the god Minos and his two brothers.

The other reference to Asterion in classical literature comes from Pausanias, a Greek traveler and geographer who lived in the second century CE. He wrote,

In the market-place of Troizenos [in Argolis] is a temple of Artemis Soteira [Savior] with images of the goddess. It was said the temple was founded and the name Soteria given by Theseus when he returned from Crete after overcoming Asterion the son of Minos. (Pausanias, Description of Greece 2.31.1)

So here, Asterion is Minos's son (and presumably the Minotaur), while the other two writers call him Minos' stepfather. This shows just how garbled and confused myths can become as they're passed down over time. Asterion's mention in Pausanias's work is the tidbit that Karl Kerenyi used to link him with the Minotaur.

Tauros Asterion's connection with both cattle (wild aurochs and domesticated cattle) and stars is quite old. The identification of the constellation Taurus as a bull goes back to the Paleolithic era, if the artwork in Lascaux cave is any indication. And there was already a bull and cow cult in western Anatolia when the Minoans' ancestors migrated from there down to the Aegean during the Neolithic era. In many cultures, spots on the hides of animals are symbols of the stars in the night sky. Minoan art includes images of spotted bulls, which could be taken to represent the starry or cosmic aspect of Tauros Asterion.

Tauros Asterion's two main aspects, the earthly and the stellar, show up in his connection with both his mother Rhea and the cosmic mother goddess Ourania. This connection with Ourania along with his immense age, going back to the Paleolithic, give Tauros Asterion a broad outlook, almost a cosmic point of view. But he's also very earthy. He understands material existence better than some other deities do. This makes him a helpful ally in dealing with practical issues, from finances to housing to health. Of course, for health matters, always seek appropriate professional (human) care, too.

Because of his understanding of the physical world and the embodied life, Tauros Asterion is the Benefactor of athletes and sports. Also, due to his bovine nature, he's the Benefactor of leatherworkers.

Thaena, Sydaili, and Eshuumna make up a special kind of triplicity of deities, as they are the Serpent Mother's children. We connected with these three deities via shared gnosis in collaboration with the Serpent Mother. As with the other mother goddesses in the pantheon, the Serpent Mother has children. We just had to find them.

Thaena (TYE-nah), Sydaili (sye-DAY-lee), and Eshuumna (eh-SHOOM-nah) are a triplicity of deities who form the Unseen Rainbow. Thaena and Sydaili are the Divine Twins, and Eshuumna stands between them. Though human gender doesn't really apply to deities, we can think of Thaena as a goddess, Sydaili as a god, and Eshuumna as a nonbinary or genderfluid deity. Each of the three can be approached separately, but the other two will always be present nearby.

Specific colors are associated with them, blue with Thaena, red with Sydaili, and rainbow (the full color spectrum, not just stripes of separate, individual colors) with Eshuumna. These three deities are also connected with the constellation Gemini. Thaena and Sydaili are the two stars known today as Alpha and Beta Geminorum, and Eshuumna can be found in the space between them.

All three of these deities can help with healing due to their Serpent nature. The Serpent Mother and her children wend their way through facets of existence that aren't easy for humans to access or understand. Serpent nature is about connecting with the different realms of being and moving through them in ways that create change.

These three are also deities of perception. Thaena is about perceiving the world through the lens of wisdom. Sydaili is about perceiving the world through the lens of joy. And Eshuumna is about perceiving the world without a lens. You need all three to perceive yourself and the world in a balanced way.

Thaena's gift of wisdom isn't just the wisdom of the leader or the diplomat, but the innate wisdom that resides deep within each of us, directing us to live our lives in a sacred way. That includes the ordinary, everyday aspects of life as well as the parts humans often label as "big" or important. Because what humans perceive as important isn't always what's truly important in the vast scheme of things.

Sydaili's gift of joy isn't necessarily a physical or sensual joy like we think of in connection with Thumia and Kaulo. Instead, it's more "essence of joy," joy for its own sake as a sacred aspect of life, where it bubbles up out of your very soul. He holds the container of safety so this kind of joy has a place to flourish.

And Eshuumna's gift of perception without a lens, of lifting the veil of our own biases and desire for denial, isn't so much about removing what isn't really there. It's more about seeing what *is* really there. And that's a powerful gift.

These deities are experiential and Mystery, and words don't quite get them across fully. Personal connection with them is the best choice for understanding them. They can be found in Minoan art wherever we see three columns together or two columns with a noticeable space between them.

These three have a focus on the metaphoric lenses through which we view the world, so they're the Benefactors of justice; not the legal system per se, which often has little to do with real justice, but integrity, honesty, fair play, and the truth that lies behind all things.

Thumia (TOO-mee-ah) is a goddess of physical pleasure and joy. She is paired with Kaulo, but like the other Minoan deities, they're not husband and wife. Thumia is a face of the goddess Therasia.

Thumia helps us find sacred joy in the pleasurable physical activities of life, from dancing to cuddles, hugs, massages, and sex. Any kind of joyous, consenting physical activity falls under her purview; not just sex, but all kinds of physical expression and connection. She also appreciates the sacredness of laughter. Although she's not as interested in bawdy humor as Kaulo is, she encourages us to find the joy in life by allowing it to bubble up as giggly laughter, the way we did so often as children. She wants us to find joy and hold onto it as we move through life.

Although we refer to Thumia as a goddess, she's a bit genderfluid. Neither she nor Kaulo fits easily into any kind of binary human category, even though we call them "god" and "goddess" for simplicity's sake. Of course, human gender doesn't really apply to the deities anyway, but we use it as a construct to help us connect with them more easily. In addition, if you think of Thumia and Kaulo as standing next to each other, you can imagine a third deity, called ThumiaKaulo, standing between them. ThumiaKaulo is a blend of the two who is both masculine and feminine at the same time. The Two imply the existence of the Third, magically speaking.

Thumia is associated with the color red, especially red sashes and hip scarves, as well as any kind of small, jingling bells, like the hip and ankle bells often worn by belly dancers. She's the Benefactor of all occupations that involve the joyful use of the body as the primary focus, from dancers to sex workers, with a special emphasis on female-presenting sex workers.

Zagreus (zah-GROOS) is a bull-god who is a face of Tauros Asterion. There's a lot of argument about the etymology of his name, which could mean anything from 'the handsome bull' to 'the dismembered one.' Don't confuse him with the Hellenic god Zeus; they're not related. The Minoan Zagreus is also substantially different from the later Orphic deity.

Zagreus is a shamanic god whose rites probably involved the sacrifice and dismemberment of bulls. The concept of dismemberment is important in shamanism, representing the transformation the spirit worker undergoes when they're symbolically taken apart and put back together again during spirit journeys. On a more mundane level, dismemberment is involved when a bull is slaughtered and cut up to be cooked, its meat consumed by humans and transformed in the process of digestion.

Zagreus is associated with the Blooming Time, since he's the bull who comes wreathed in flowers in the spring. The Blooming Time is a season when life and death intertwine, a time of flowers blooming and grain crops cut down in harvest, a time of joyous preparation for sailing season and the not-so-joyous culling of the herds. Zagreus treads the line between life and death, as shamanic deities do, reminding us that they're two sides of the same coin.

The Blooming Time Bull who comes wreathed in flowers during the season when life and death intertwine is the Benefactor of the professions that unite the living and the dead: coroners, medical examiners, funeral directors, and related occupations.

Chapter 4

The Sacred Calendar:
Myth Entwined in the Year

The sacred calendar I'm about to share with you is one we've developed in Ariadne's Tribe. We've pieced it together via a combination of Minoan art, archaeology, dance ethnology, archaeoastronomy and comparative mythology from the fragments of information available to us. It's probably an oversimplified version of the one the Minoans used. Like so many other ancient cultures, their year was likely full of many, many festivals, both small local celebrations and bigger ones that encompassed the whole island, some celebrated by everyone and others celebrated only by particular professions or portions of society.

The ancient Minoan sacred calendar was rooted in the natural seasonal cycles of the Mediterranean region where the island of Crete is located. As I explained in the chapter about Minoan history, the Mediterranean climate is unique and is different from the four-season cycle of spring, summer, autumn, and winter. The mild, rainy winter was the busy agricultural season for Minoan farmers, while the hot, dry, rainless summer was the "dead" time when the fields lay fallow.

In addition to the farmers, on Crete there were also sailors along the coastline and goat-herders in the mountains. All three of these subcultures had their own ways of celebrating the changing seasons. But all three lived in harmony with the cycles of the Mediterranean climate.

In the Tribe, we divide the Mediterranean year into three seasons: Summer, Winter, and the Blooming Time. This is a system we developed via folklore, comparative mythology, and historical research. During the Summer, the sailing folk went to sea to make their living. The farmers rested as their fields lay bare, too hot and dry to grow any field crops. And the herders took their animals up to the high summer pastures in the mountains, where the springs and streams fed by snowmelt still supported some fresh green growth the animals could eat.

Then the rainy season began in the time we might call autumn, and Summer shifted into Winter. The farmers plowed the newly-softened ground and planted their crops, which grew throughout the mild season. The sailors came home and docked their boats as the winds changed and became dangerous. The Winter was the sailors' "fallow season." And the herders brought their animals down from the mountains to the now-green lowlands to graze.

Summer and Winter were long, each taking up almost half the year. That leaves a small portion of the year in the springtime, two to three months we call the Blooming Time. It's a beautiful season in Crete, with huge swaths of wildflowers blooming across the lowlands and sweeping up into the foothills of the mountains. But it was also a busy season in ancient Crete.

The sailing people spent this short season bringing their ships out of the storage sheds, repairing them, and getting ready for their summertime voyages. The farmers harvested their fields of grain (wheat, barley, and rye), ageing it for a number of days then threshing and winnowing it to store for later use. And the herders had the difficult task of culling their herds, slaughtering the older and weaker animals since the high summer pastures weren't as lush as the lowland winter ones.

So the Blooming Time was a season of life and death intertwined, of vigorous spring growth as well as harvest and slaughter. It was a concentrated, focused pivot on which the larger seasons of Summer and Winter hinged.

Within these seasons lie a series of festivals we celebrate as part of modern Minoan spiritual practice. The celebrations in the sacred calendar are intertwined with the Minoan mythos. In other words, the mythic tales take place at specific times of the year, from Ariadne and Dionysus's sacred marriage at Midsummer to Ariadne's rise to the World Above during the Mysteries in the autumn to Therasia's self-rebirth at Midwinter, and more. As the year unrolls, so do the stories of the family of deities.

As I noted above, the planting and harvest times in the Mediterranean are reversed from those in four-season climates. If you live in a Mediterranean climate (southern California, for instance) feel free to celebrate those festivals based on the Mediterranean seasons, as they're written here. But if you live elsewhere, it's perfectly all right to switch the planting and harvest celebrations to the times that fit your local climate. This is a nature-based religion, so respecting the natural cycles where you live is encouraged.

Minoan culture lasted for centuries, during which time Minoan religion grew and evolved. Like the Egyptians, they tended to add on new layers without removing the old, so by the end it was quite a textured tradition. In the Tribe, we've chosen our mythos as "snapshots" from multiple eras, seeking a balance between the old and the new and maintaining respect for all the deities throughout.

The Blessing of the Ships

Third Monday in May

Boats and ships were a major part of Minoan culture, which makes sense given Crete is an island. The Minoans traded not only on Crete itself but all around the Mediterranean and possibly out into the Atlantic as well. They caught the fish and seafood that were such a large part of their diet. And they built port cities that ringed Crete, with harbors to dock at and ship sheds to store their sailing vessels during the off season.

The Blessing of the Ships celebrates the beginning of sailing season in late spring. Fragments of Bronze Age tradition preserved in classical-era writings combined with archaeoastronomy research set the date at the heliacal rising of the Pleiades, which would have taken place in mid-May during the Bronze Age. We've chosen the third Monday in May as an approximation of that date, but also because it's a (forgive me) floating holiday.

We don't know for certain what the Minoans did to bless their ships before setting sail each season. They may have held a large waterborne festival like the one depicted on the Flotilla fresco from Akrotiri and like are still held around the Mediterranean today. They would certainly have called on Grandmother Ocean for blessings and safety as they set out onto the water. Perhaps they made offerings to her, tossing garlands and wreaths of fresh flowers into the water and decorating their boats with flowers, as some seagoing cultures still do today.

Most people don't have boats today. But in the northern hemisphere, the Blessing of the Ships falls at the beginning of summer vacation season. In the Tribe, we take this opportunity to ritually bless our vehicles, especially if we plan to make long journeys.

Summer Weaving

24 May to 17 June (exact dates may shift if Solstice is not on 21 June)

This is the season that leads up to Summer Solstice, a time to contemplate the connections that weave the living and the dead, the human and the divine into one great Tapestry of Being. The golden thread that twists through the Labyrinth winds through our lives as well, our joy reverberating out into the greater weave. During Summer Weaving we celebrate these connections, acknowledging our part in the greater tapestry and recognizing that our actions have repercussions on all the others: humans, deities, ancestors, the inspirited world.

71

Summer Weaving is celebrated every fourth day leading up to Summer Solstice. Assuming Solstice falls on 21 June, which is its most typical date, the days of Summer Weaving are as follows:

24 May
28 May
1 June
5 June
9 June
13 June
17 June

On each of these days, we take time out to perform some activity that helps us focus on our interconnection with the rest of existence. This could mean offering to the ancestors, learning about the environmental web of life, noticing what plants and local foods are in season where we live, or walking a labyrinth while focusing on the sacred golden thread that connects us all. As Summer Weaving progresses, we can feel our connection with the solstice growing ever closer.

The Height of Summer

Summer Solstice, approximately 21 June (exact date varies from year to year)

There are two layers of mythos at the Summer Solstice. On this day, the sun goddess Therasia is at the height of her power, her intense heat and light beating down on the Earth during long days, with the short nights bringing little relief. Remember, the summer is the "dead season" in the Mediterranean, with no rain in sight and immense heat everywhere. At Summer Solstice, we stand in awe of Therasia's power, the force that drives the life on our planet. The Minoans made pilgrimages

72

up the mountainsides and lit bonfires on the mountaintops, at the dozens of peak sanctuaries across Crete, to celebrate the solstices. They probably also sang and danced, performed rituals, and made offerings on the plazas in front of the peak sanctuary buildings. These are all activities that modern Pagans can perform, even if we don't have access to peak sanctuaries.

In addition to the sun goddess's annual cycle, at Midsummer we also focus on the Confluence of Dionysus and Ariadne. In the Tribe pantheon, they aren't husband and wife but are independent, each complete within themselves. At this time of year, Dionysus is in the World Above and Ariadne is in the Underworld. They come together in a place outside of space and time, perhaps we could call it the mythic realm, to weave together complementary (not binary) forces: gender, the many worlds, even life and death. Their union creates beauty, love, and hope. And then they part ways, turning back to their individual responsibilities, until the next Midsummer.

Architectural alignments and Minoan art suggest that rituals and mystery plays at the temples were aspects of the Summer Solstice celebrations in Minoan Crete. Even if we modern Pagans don't have big temples, we can still celebrate with our own rituals, and even with mystery plays if we gather a few people together.

The Summer Serpent Days

Late June / early July
The Summer Serpent Days, the days between the Summer Solstice and the Water Mirror, are a special time. Because the Water Mirror (see below) takes place on the first full moon following the Summer Solstice, the number of days between the two events varies from year to year. The movable lunar cycle slithers like a serpent around the steady points in the solar calendar. We might think of the days between Summer Solstice

and the Water Mirror as intercalary days, days that belong neither to the half-year that has just ended nor to the one that's about to start. A time out of time, slinking its way between the parts of the calendar, shifting in size from one year to the next, but always magical and special. This is an excellent time for reflection on the previous half-year and divination for the half-year to come, particularly regarding connections with others, whether human or divine.

The Water Mirror

First Full Moon after Summer Solstice

This is a celebration of the reflections in life, the light and fluid aspects of experience. The full moons immediately following the Summer and Winter Solstice were key points in the octaeteris, one of the sacred calendars the Minoans used. As I mentioned earlier, in the octaeteris, eight solar years coincide with 99 lunations, a dance of sun and moon. Water mirrors have a long history, with evidence for their use going back at least as far as the Neolithic. To celebrate this festival, we make a water mirror that reflects the sun at midday and drop a small offering item in it, making sure we never look at our own reflection in the water. Some people like to scry in the water once it has stilled after dropping the offering item in. We dispose of the water and the offering by pouring them into a larger body of water (a lake or river, for instance) or by leaving the bowl out until after sunset and then pouring the water and the offering onto the ground.

Feast of Grapes

31 August

As you might guess, the Feast of Grapes focuses on Dionysus, the God of the Vine. This is the time of the grape harvest, when the ripe fruit is picked to make into wine. Dionysus is embodied in the grapevine and the fruit, so the harvest is his death, when he descends to the Underworld. This gives his worshipers access to that realm for healing and communion with the spirits of the dead.

Just like other harvest festivals in the ancient world, the date would have varied from year to year depending on when the crop was ready to harvest. We've chosen a date that fits within the usual time range for ripening grapes in the temperate areas of the northern hemisphere. If you have a grapevine, you could choose to celebrate whenever your grapes are ripe, even if it isn't on 31 August.

It's likely the Minoans celebrated the grape harvest in the vineyards. This may have involved clergy blessing the crop and the people making ritual libations, perhaps of the previous year's wine. A small batch of the year's grape harvest may have been ceremonially stomped into juice during the celebrations, though the majority of it probably would have waited for later, since it's a laborious task. And the day, or possibly multiple days, of this festival would surely have involved feasting and dancing.

In the Tribe, we dance and feast and make offerings to Dionysus at this festival. We also take the opportunity to perform divination, typically by scrying in cups or bowls of wine.

The Mysteries

1 through 10 September

The Eleusinian Mysteries, or some early variant of them, may have originated on Crete. With this possibility in mind, we celebrate a Minoan version of the Mysteries every year. The earliest known beginning and ending dates for the Eleusinian Mysteries were based on the heliacal rising of the stars Arcturus and Spica. We've set our festival on the calendar dates when those risings occurred during the Bronze Age.

In the Minoan version of the Mysteries, Rhea is the Great Mother and Ariadne is the Daughter who descends to the Underworld during the "dead time" of year, which, if you'll recall, is the summer in the Mediterranean. Ariadne isn't abducted; she willingly descends to the World Below so she can lovingly care for the spirits of the dead. She's the Queen of the Dead, and also the Queen Bee: the head of the Melissae, the bee-spirit goddesses who care for the spirits of the dead when Ariadne isn't there. They surround and support her in her work to aid the spirits. In addition, the goddess Eileithyia is Ariadne's torch-bearer during her annual sojourn in the Underworld.

Once the summer ends and the rains begin, Rhea has Iacchus (young Dionysus) lead her down to the Underworld to let her daughter know it's time to return to the World Above. Rhea has missed Ariadne but hasn't been tormented by her loss, because her daughter was never lost, but had simply gone to a known place to take care of some of her responsibilities. Since time passes differently in the Underworld than it does in the World Above, Rhea needs to tell Ariadne when it's time to return.

Ariadne returns to the World Above with the first green sprouts in the autumn fields. She spends the growing season among the living as the embodiment of the grain crop. Then she dies at the grain harvest and returns to the Underworld to start the cycle again.

The Mysteries are a reminder that the cycle of being is just that, a cycle, not a linear process. The soul continues onward from one lifetime to another, held in love by Ariadne and the Melissae between incarnations. The agricultural cycle and the process of reincarnation are two reflections of the same concept, life turning and returning in a never-ending sacred circle.

The Minoans probably performed elaborate mystery plays and extensive rituals over the course of the multi-day festival, precursors to the famed Eleusinian Mysteries many centuries later in mainland Greece. Modern life doesn't typically allow that kind of activity for most Pagans. Still, a simple mystery play is feasible for small groups, on either the first or the last day of the Mysteries. And individuals can make offerings of grain and pomegranates and meditate on the ineffable Mysteries of life, death, and beyond.

The New Year

Autumn Equinox, approximately 21 September (exact date varies from year to year)
In the Mediterranean, the rains begin around this time of year; the soil softens and the farmers plant their crops. It's the beginning of the agricultural cycle, much like the farmers of northern Europe who celebrated their new year in the spring when they sowed their fields. Archaeoastronomy and comparative mythology suggest the Minoans began their year with the planting time in the autumn.

Astronomical alignments on buildings on Crete, from the earliest tombs to the biggest temples, suggest the Autumn Equinox as the formal date for the new year. In the countryside, people would have celebrated whenever the experienced farmers decided the ground was soft and moist enough to plow and plant. But at the temples, it's likely a specific date was set so plans could be made in advance.

The festivities would have taken place outdoors, in the fields, whether those belonged to individual farmers or the big temples. This is the time of preparation for Ariadne's return to the World Above, a joyful celebration of the renewal of life. For the first time in months, the countryside is green and lush again, with new plants growing.

Dancing in the fields wearing wreaths and crowns of fresh greenery is one way to celebrate this festival. For a simpler version, choose a few seeds to plant in a pot, maybe some herbs to grow on your windowsill, and watch new life be reborn as the green sprouts push their way up through the soil, like Ariadne rising back into our world.

Harbor Home

Third Monday in October
While the Blessing of the Ships opens the Mediterranean sailing season, Harbor Home closes it. This is the time of year when all the ships that had been on short or long voyages would return to their home ports for the winter, bringing the news of foreign lands with them.

While the Blessing of the Ships falls around the date when the heliacal rising of the Pleiades would have occurred during the Bronze Age, Harbor Home takes place at the heliacal setting of that constellation. This is the time of year when the winds change, making sailing increasingly more hazardous. So the sailors and traders would bring their ships home and stay in port until the following spring, when it was time to start the cycle all over again.

In Minoan times, Harbor Home probably lasted a number of days as the ships and boats returned one by one from nearby and faraway voyages at the end of the sailing season. When they were all back, each port town or city would have had its own celebration. Having a date by which all the ships would arrive back home would have provided a sense of security for the families in port, knowing when to expect their loved ones' return. It's likely that a considerable portion of the Minoan population went to sea every year, so the Blessing of the Ships and Harbor Home would have been important points in the year for coastal settlements.

In addition to the ships returning with their crews and trade goods, they would also have returned with news. Most of it would have been welcome, but each year, there would have been people who left at the Blessing of the Ships and didn't make it back home. So Harbor Home would also have been a bittersweet time, and a time of profound relief for those families whose loved ones did return.

It's likely the Minoans made offerings of thanksgiving to Posidaeja when the ships came home. That's something we can do for this festival as modern Pagans. The offerings might also include remembrances for those who passed away during the sailing season. We can also take this opportunity to "decommission" vehicles, not just boats but also cars, bicycles, and so on. This is another funereal aspect to this festival, since we name boats and many of us name our other vehicles as well.

Therasia's Labor

16 November to 19 December (exact dates may shift if Solstice is not on 21 December)
Instead of a single day, Therasia's labor is a sacred season, a time of expectant waiting, reflection, and preparation for the arrival of Winter Solstice. Liturgical seasons leading up to sacred days are far older than Christianity. And both archaeoastronomy and comparative mythology tell us the Winter Solstice was a major focal point of Minoan religion.

The Solstice is a solar festival, based on the sun's annual cycle. So Therasia is at the center of it, with her rebirth happening on the Solstice itself (see below). The season of Therasia's Labor helps us focus on the way the solar year is slowing down before it comes to a metaphorical stop at Midwinter, then starts up again for the new cycle of Therasia's death and rebirth, which frame the moment of sunrise on Midwinter morning.

The concept of labor and birth is also reflected in the other set of mythos associated with Midwinter, the story of Rhea giving birth to the Divine Child Dionysus on Midwinter morning. Our research suggests the Winter Solstice mythos surrounding the Sun Goddess is older than the Earth Mother mythos for the same day. But Minoan religion added layer upon layer over the centuries of Minoan civilization, so we acknowledge both at Midwinter. However, since Therasia's tale is probably the older one, we've named the season in her honor.

The name "Therasia's Labor" and the pattern of the sacred days within this holy season were created by Tribe member Forrest Novawynd, with Therasia's inspiration. Therasia's Labor begins in mid-November and is celebrated on seven separate days leading up to Solstice. These days fall in a pattern, coming closer and closer together as Solstice approaches, in much the same way contractions get closer and closer together during labor. Here's the pattern, assuming Solstice falls on 21 December. If it falls on 20 or 22 December, as it does some years, you would shift all the dates forward or back by one.

> November 16
>   wait 7 days
> November 24
>   wait 6 days
> December 1
>   wait 5 days
> December 7
>   wait 4 days
> December 12
>   wait 3 days
> December 16
>   wait 2 days
> December 19
>   wait 1 day
> WINTER SOLSTICE

The activities for the marked days during this season should involve light in one way or another. You could frame each day by watching the sunrise and sunset. You could light an oil lamp or candle before dawn and/or after sunset. Or you could stand beneath the sun at noon, perhaps in the Minoan salute posture. As Therasia's Labor progresses, you can feel the Solstice drawing ever closer.

The Depths of Winter

Winter Solstice, approximately 21 December (exact date varies from year to year)
Like the Summer Solstice, the Winter Solstice has two layers of mythos, involving Therasia, Rhea, and Dionysus. In the Depths of Winter, the mythic symbolism is of birth and rebirth, the end of one cycle and the beginning of another. And both myths involve sacred caves.

The height of Therasia's power was at Summer Solstice, when her heat powered down on the Earth; now she's so weak, she retreats to her cave to hide, to die and be reborn like the Phoenix rising from its own ashes. On Midwinter morning, within her cave she dies to herself in the last dark moment before dawn then arises from her cave at the first moment of sunrise, shining with new life.

Winter Solstice is also the time when Rhea retreats to her cave to give birth to Dionysus, the Divine Child. Dionysus isn't a sun god; instead, he's a year-king, the embodiment of the cycle of the solar year. Rhea labors through the night on Midwinter eve, and at sunrise on Winter Solstice morning, the Divine Child is born.

Winter Solstice astronomical alignments in the Knossos Throne Room suggest Midwinter sunrise was a time of sacred ritual there. And the griffins on the frescoes suggest a connection with Therasia. Maybe the Minoans kept vigil all night, waiting for the sunrise and the sacred birth and rebirth. An all-night vigil is one possibility for a modern celebration of Winter Solstice. But simply getting up before sunrise to witness the sun coming over the horizon, followed by offerings and celebrations, would also be fitting.

The Winter Serpent Days

Late December / early January
The Winter Serpent Days, the days between the Winter Solstice and the Blessing of the Waters, are similar to the Summer Serpent Days, their number changing from year to year, a time out of time, the half-year turning on its hinge. This is an excellent time for reflection on the previous half-year and divination for the half-year to come, particularly regarding anything you might begin or "birth" during the upcoming half-year.

The Blessing of the Waters

First Full Moon after Winter Solstice
This festival is based on a folk practice that has survived as a local Christian holy day on Crete. Dance ethnology research suggests this was originally both a blessing of the spirits of bodies of water as well as a time to celebrate the coming of age of young men and possibly to choose one young man for religious office.

This festival is typical of the many smaller celebrations that probably peppered the Minoan sacred calendar in between the bigger solstice and equinox celebrations. Even though the Minoans had advanced water systems (aqueducts, enclosed sewers, canals, cisterns, even manual-flush toilets) water was still a precious substance. It still had to be carried in buckets to wherever it was needed in the temple, in the home, or on the farm. And if the mountain springs that fed the aqueducts dried up, fresh water could become dangerously scarce.

The Blessing of the Waters is a time to give thanks for water and to connect with our local natural fresh water in whatever form it might take: stream, pond, lake, river, even rainwater we've collected. We can make offerings of incense and song, and we can touch the water to connect with it both physically and spiritually.

For a coming-of-age ceremony for boys, this festival involves a parent or spiritual leader tossing a labrys into the water. The boy must leap into the water and retrieve the labrys, bringing it back to shore. To choose a young man for religious office, multiple young men enter the water once the labrys has been tossed in. The one who can retrieve it and bring it back to shore is the one chosen for the office. Of course, if you live where January is very cold, take all appropriate precautions before anyone goes in the water, and be sure to have warm, dry clothing available immediately afterward. This is meant to be a simple contest, not a dangerous ordeal.

The Harvest

Spring Equinox, approximately 21 March (exact date varies from year to year)
The grain the farmers sowed in their fields last autumn, when the rainy season began, has grown throughout the mild winter and is now ready to harvest. Ariadne has spent the growing season in the World Above as the grain sprouted, grew, and ripened. Now she dies with the harvest and descends to the Underworld until next autumn, as the people give thanks to her and to the ancestors for an abundant harvest that will sustain them for the coming year.

The actual harvest activities would have taken place on the farms whenever the grain was ripe, a date that would have varied from year to year. But as with the agricultural new year in the autumn, there were probably official celebrations at the

83

temples on the equinox itself. There are astronomical alignments to the equinoxes at many Minoan temples and shrines.

Harvest isn't a single act. Between the cutting of the ripe grain stalks in the fields and the storing of the finished kernels in stone silos come other activities: aging the grain so it's all dry and can easily be removed from the stalks, then threshing and winnowing it. These activities were every bit as sacred as the first cut into the stalks during harvest and the final closing of the storehouse door. Humans or animals, or both, trod the harvest on the circular threshing floors, breaking the grain off the stalks. Then with baskets and woven fans, the people blew the husks off, leaving the individual kernels bare and ready for storage. Then, when the work was done, the celebration could begin.

Dance ethnology and anthropology research suggest that many of the circular folk dances from Crete and other areas around the Mediterranean began on those ancient threshing floors. So dancing and singing are appropriate activities for this festival, as are offerings to Ariadne and to the ancestors. Astronomical building alignments suggest the Minoans held communal feasts at the tombs at harvest time. Baking some bread and sharing it with family and friends in honor of the Beloved Dead would be a good modern adaptation of this activity, being sure, of course, to give the first bit of fresh-baked bread to the ancestors as an offering.

The Blooming Time

The days between Spring Equinox and the Blessing of the Ships

The Blooming Time is a short, unique, and beautiful season when life and death intertwine. Although flowers bloom throughout the year on Crete, the profusion of wildflowers in the Blooming

Time underscores the importance of fresh flowers as a symbol of the intertwining of life and death; pick a flower, and it will soon wither.

The Blooming Time was an important time of year to all three subcultures of Minoan Crete: the sailors, the farmers, and the herders. For the sailors, it was the time to prepare for the upcoming sailing season, make any last-minute repairs, ready the ships, and gather the crew. For the farmers, it was the end of their busy season, the time when the grain had been harvested and was being threshed and winnowed in preparation for storage. It was the time to measure the grain and hope the harvest was big enough to last a full year. And for the goat-herders, it was the time to cull the weak and old members of the herd before moving the animals to the higher summer pastures where water would still be available.

So the Blooming Time was a season in which life and death intertwined, the vigorous spring growth as well as harvest and slaughter. It was a concentrated, focused pivot on which the larger seasons of Summer and Winter hinged.

In modern Minoan spiritual practice, we focus on the ancestors and the bull-god Zagreus at this time of year. We usually mark this season with a ritual that includes sacrificial offerings; not animal sacrifice, obviously, but the kinds of offerings that really feel like we're giving up something. The specific day for the ritual isn't as important as the focus on the meaning of the season, the proximity of life and death. Offerings and other sacred activities can also be spread out throughout this short season. The life/death aspect of the season makes the dark moon (the new moon, in other words, the days when the moon isn't visible in the night sky) a good choice for ritual activities. And, of course, fresh flowers are a part of our Blooming Time rituals, as both decorations and offerings.

You've probably noticed that many of the entries in this chapter included information about performing rituals for the various sacred festivals. How can you incorporate Minoan ritual into your own spiritual practice? And what might a modern-day Minoan ritual look like? Head on to the next chapter to find out.

Chapter 5

Ritual Format and Practices

When we began trying to figure out what kind of ritual format we wanted for Ariadne's Tribe, we looked to the Bronze Age Mediterranean, the time and place the Minoans lived, for inspiration. Though we can identify the Minoans' sacred spaces (temples, cave shrines, peak sanctuaries, home altars) and we have some idea of the general activities that went on in many of those places, we don't know the full details of how the Minoans worshiped.

As I mentioned earlier, Minoan art shows "snapshots" of several different kinds of ritual activities. Processions, offerings, and libations figure prominently in the art. Archaeologists have uncovered hundreds of libation pitchers and votive (offering) figurines as well as evidence of bonfires at a number of Minoan sacred sites. We have a good idea where the deities fit in the Minoan worldview. And we know about the religious practices of other Bronze Age cultures around the Mediterranean like the Egyptians, the Canaanites, the Sumerians and the Babylonians. The eastern Mediterranean was one great big cultural exchange area during the Bronze Age, so all the societies in the area shared many similar religious practices.

From all these tidbits of information, we created a ritual format that harks back to Minoan religion but that also works well for us as modern Pagans. This is where reconstructionism and revivalism meet, in taking the evidence we have from ancient times and turning it into a practice that can be performed in the modern world.

In this chapter, I'll share two types of ritual and a third kind of sacred activity as well. The first ritual type is the general format we use for group and solitary rituals. Of course, there will be times when you don't want to do anything as complicated as a full ritual. Simple prayer and meditation doesn't require a full-blown ritual. You can make casual offerings at any time, with no fuss and minimal preparation. But sometimes you want to go to the effort of a full ritual. Maybe you want to mark a seasonal celebration or a milestone in your life. That's what the ritual format is for.

The second ritual I'll share below is called Confluence. It's a rite of joining and connection, either temporary or long-term, and has many uses. It can be a stand-alone rite, but it can also be added to the Listening portion of the standard ritual format in a longer ceremony.

The third kind of sacred activity was an important aspect of ancient Minoan religion: offerings. There's a formal Offering section in the ritual structure below. But like the ancient Minoans, many of us like to make offerings outside of ritual. I've shared some typical methods we use that are inspired by the evidence we have for the way the Minoans practiced their religion, along with some of the specific offerings the deities enjoy.

Just like with cooking, it's good ritual practice to read the "recipe" all the way through before you begin, several times if necessary, until you really understand it. Take your time gathering any necessary supplies and preparing, so you'll have a positive experience. Now let's begin with the general-purpose ritual format.

Ariadne's Tribe Ritual Format

The ritual format is divided into six parts: Preparing, Inviting, Welcoming, Offering, Listening, and Returning. This format works for both solitary and group rituals. For group rituals, feel free to share out the parts in whatever way works for the people involved. For solitary rituals, the person performing the rite does all the parts themselves. It isn't complicated, and it works well for any number of people.

We consider accessibility to be part of the Minoan worldview of sharing, community, and helping each other. It's OK to make modifications to the ritual format to accommodate accessibility issues as long as you don't omit any of the six major sections. And signing is a perfectly acceptable method of performing any of the parts in a Tribe ritual, including all the chants. Be sure to provide seating around the ritual space for anyone who needs it. It's all right if all the participants sit during a ritual.

You might find some aspects of this ritual structure to be different from other Pagan rituals you've experienced. It doesn't involve casting a circle or otherwise separating the ritual space from "mundane" space because all space is sacred. In modern Minoan ritual, the presence of the deities purifies and consecrates the ritual area. There's a sense in which the Three Mothers (the goddesses Rhea, Therasia, and Posidaeja) *are* the temple.

This format also doesn't involve calling the quarters or watchtowers or otherwise marking the cardinal directions. These practices entered Wicca and other modern traditions via ceremonial magic, which has its roots in the classical era, dating to many centuries after the Bronze Age. There's no evidence for this kind of activity in Minoan religion. At first archaeologists thought the Minoans aligned their temples to the four cardinal directions. But it turns out they actually aligned them to astronomical events like sunrise, moonrise, and the heliacal rising of certain stars. Likewise, the four classical elements (earth, air, fire, and water) also date to long after the Bronze Age. This ritual format is based on elements that can be found in Bronze Age practices, either in Minoan art and archaeology or from comparable Bronze Age cultures around the Mediterranean.

Rather than invoking the deities, we simply invite them. It's more respectful to politely ask the deities if they'd like to join us rather than calling them in a way that could be construed as ordering them around.

We also don't usually share food during our rituals. The exception might be a special dining rite to honor the ancestors, like the one in *Ariadne's Thread*. But otherwise, we save our feasting for after the cleanup is done. Sharing a meal is a great way to ground and center after a ritual and is also a wonderful way to continue the connection of community once the ritual is over.

Speaking of the ritual being over, cleaning up from the ritual is a part of the sacred process. We don't normally discuss what we experienced during the ritual until we've at least dismantled the altar, disposed of the offerings appropriately, and put away any loose items we were using for the ritual. If you're performing ritual away from home, like at a public park, cleaning up consists of packing everything away so it's ready to take home.

Cleaning up and dismantling the altar helps to ground out the energy from the ritual so we can return from the sacred space renewed and ready to function in our regular lives once again. It's lovely to have a group meal or social gathering with snacks after cleaning up, to ground yourselves and have a dedicated time to share and discuss what you experienced during the ritual. Even if you're doing a solitary ritual, it's nice to take your time cleaning up and putting everything away, then sit down to have a grounding meal or a snack and a drink and contemplate what you've just experienced.

Please remember that every ritual needs a sacred purpose or goal. Don't perform a ritual as a joke or just because it's a certain date or moon phase. Think about why you're doing what you're doing. If you're "simply" celebrating the season, then focus on that concept thoughtfully as you perform the ritual. Be mindful and present to the sacredness and the joy of what you're doing. This will help deepen your experience and develop your relationships with the deities.

That was a lot of *don'ts*. I'm not trying to discourage you, but simply to put these ritual practices into the context of the kinds of activities many modern Pagans are familiar with, and show you the differences. How about we move onto some *do's* now?

This ritual structure is designed to be used by both groups and solitaries. If you're performing a ritual solo, simply speak, perform, or chant all the parts yourself. If you're a member of a group performing the ritual, you can share out the parts however you like. There's no requirement to have a "congregation" or audience for any ritual. But if there are people who don't want to take on a formal role, they can simply participate as observers. That's OK, too.

The basics you'll need for ritual are an altar, a side table, and some sort of figurine for each of the deities you're honoring. The altar can be a table or other surface (a shelf or fireplace mantel, for instance) that will hold the items you'll be focusing on in the ritual. The side table is for the "extra" items: the offerings (before they're given to the deities), any props you might be using if you're performing a mystery play, matches or lighters, and anything else that doesn't belong on the altar but that you'll need during the ritual.

You may enjoy decorating your altar to match the theme of the ritual, whether it's a season you're celebrating or some other focus like a rite of passage. Flowers, ribbons, altar cloths, and other colorful and thematic items can help set the tone for the ritual. We don't typically light candles as part of the ritual process, but you can certainly include candles on the altar to add to the ambience if you like. If you want to hark back to Minoan times, you could use oil lamps instead, the small ceramic kind that was common in antiquity, since the Minoans lived before candles were invented.

It's not necessary to perform any kind of ritual cleansing beforehand. But it is a good idea to have recently bathed and wear clean clothing, both for hygiene and to show respect for the ritual process and the deities and humans who will be joining you in the temple space. We reserve incense for offerings and don't use it for cleansing. So if you want to do some kind of ritual cleansing of yourself, the other participants, and/or your ritual area before you begin, asperging (sprinkling) with spring water or herb-infused water is a good choice.

The Three Mothers are always invited into every ritual, but you don't always need to include figurines for them. If other deities will be the focus of the ritual, you can choose to use figurines just for those deities, Dionysus at the Feast of Grapes, for instance. And when I say "figurine," I mean any small object that evokes the deity to you. It doesn't have to be a human-shaped statue. For example, you might choose a large seashell to represent Posidaeja or a potted plant to represent Rhea. If it will fit on the altar and it evokes the presence of the deity to you, then use it.

Speaking of the altar, the deity figurines don't begin there. Instead, we bring them in during the opening procession. Each figurine is carried into the ritual space by a person who performs all the actions for that figurine during the course of the rite. For solitary ritual, we put all the figurines in one basket or on one tray and bring them in together. In a group ritual, ideally each figurine is carried by a separate person. If you don't have enough people to do that, then simply share out the figurines in whatever way works best for your group.

Instead of carrying the figurines in our bare hands, we set them in baskets or on wooden trays and cover them with cloths. They are uncovered, brought into the sacred space, and placed on the altar as part of the ritual activities. Then the process is reversed to end the ritual, with the figurines being removed from the altar, covered, and carried out. Since the figurines don't begin on the altar, be sure to leave space for them when you're setting up the altar and decorating it.

One of our common practices involves embodying a deity during the ritual. This doesn't necessarily mean trance possession, though it does appear from the art the Minoans did that on a regular basis. I don't recommend trying it without proper training, though. In its simplest form, embodying a deity simply means speaking on their behalf, perhaps as part of a mystery play or a guided meditation. It's not a requirement and isn't appropriate for every ritual. But when I mention below "people embodying deities," that's what I mean.

Music is also an important part of ritual. In addition to beginning and ending the ritual with three sounds from a musical instrument such as a drum or a triton trumpet, we also chant during the procession into the ritual space, during the Offering portion of the ritual, and during the procession out of the ritual space. The words to those three chants are included below. Videos of the chants are available in the Ariadne's Tribe playlist on my YouTube channel.

Because Ariadne's Tribe is a non-hierarchical spiritual tradition, we don't have titles like High Priestess or High Priest. Instead, we use the term "clergy" or "officiant" to refer to the people who have active roles in any given ritual. This is a temporary, ritual-specific title and doesn't apply anywhere else. The Minoans, of course, had permanent professional clergy in their temples. But we've chosen not to mirror that aspect of Minoan culture. This makes it easier for us to build egalitarian community and to share the joy of participating in ritual with as many people as possible.

Though you may find some of the details to be new and different, I think the overall ritual format will feel familiar. There's a time of preparation, an invitation to the deities and welcoming them into the ritual space, making offerings to them, listening to what they have to say to us, thanking them, and returning to the Big World carrying the blessings we received in the ritual. Now that we have those preliminaries out of the way, let's have a look at the ritual format itself.

Preparing

This section prepares both the people and the space for the ritual. We "awaken" and open the space, the people, and the ritual items to the presence of the divine so all of these together can welcome the deities. We do this whether we're putting on the ritual in a permanent temple, shrine, or altar space or in a temporary ritual area like a public park. Your altar and side table should already be set up, and the whole ritual space should already be prepared before you begin.

The practical aspects of Preparing are pretty simple. They involve the participants lining up outside the sacred space to get ready for the procession, then having everyone take a few moments to calm and focus their minds on the sacred task at hand. I like to remind everyone to silence their phones at this point. I usually do this with a gently humorous comment such as, "Now let's all turn our phones to their most reverent setting, which is *off*." It's OK to bring electronic devices into ritual space, including to use them to read the ritual from. Just be sure they don't make any noises that might interrupt the activities.

The "lineup" for the procession is simple; people who will embody deities and those carrying deity figurines go first, followed by any others who have parts in the ritual. After them, everyone else can arrange themselves in whatever order suits their fancy. Be sure your deity figurines are covered before you begin. The Three Mothers (Rhea, Therasia, and Posidaeja) and their figurines have precedence, so they go ahead of any other deities you might be including. Again, you don't *have* to include figurines for the Three Mothers if they're not the focus of the ritual, but you can if you like.

When everyone is in line, focused, and ready, begin with Honoring the Metal. Although metal is really ordinary to us in the modern world, in the Bronze Age it was still something of a small miracle. Metal is the Mothers' gift to humanity, so we begin our rituals by acknowledging the sacredness of all metals, from iron and bronze to gold and silver.

Metals can be a great help to us, but these gifts from the Mothers have also been exploited in ways that are disrespectful and damaging to the Earth as well as being used to harm our fellow human beings and the rest of the world. This part of the ritual is a reminder to respect and honor this gift and use it to create positive change in our own lives. Honoring the Metals allows us to think about these ideas regarding the metal we bring into ritual space as well as all the other metal in our lives. One of the officiants says the following while everyone else listens:

> We acknowledge all the metal we wear, carry, and bring into the temple as the Mother Goddess Rhea's precious gift to humankind. Every piece of metal we use is her child. Let us always remember that.

Everyone should be calm, quiet, and ready to focus on the ritual before you move on to the next section.

Inviting

This part of the ritual sends out an invitation to the deities to join us. Of course, there's a sense in which they're always with us. But this process invites them to be with us in a more focused way, on both our part and theirs. It opens a particular kind of conversation between us and them that plays out in the process of the ritual. This is the beginning of that process.

Once everyone is lined up and focused, but before you begin the procession, start the ritual by sounding a musical instrument three times. The Minoans had triton trumpets, and this is my favorite way of beginning a ritual. Three blasts on the trumpet will definitely raise goosebumps in the participants. But triton trumpets can be hard to come by. Thankfully, rattling a sistrum in three short bursts or striking three blows on a hand drum also works just fine. Just don't use a solid metal gong or bell to begin the ritual unless Therasia is the only deity being honored in the rite, since those instruments are sacred to her. Sometimes we choose other instruments depending on the deity who's the focus of the ritual. Dionysus, for instance, enjoys the tambourine. And Thumia and Kaulo are especially fond of hip and ankle bells. But drums and sistrums are the basic go-to instruments to begin and end rituals, and they'll work regardless of which deities you're inviting.

Once you've sounded your instrument three times, uncover the figurines and invite the deities to join you. The people who are carrying the deity figurines should hold onto the covers for now. The Mothers are always invited in first, even if other deities will be the focus of the rite, and even if you aren't using figurines for them, because they're the foundation of the temple and our family of deities. To invite the deities, say the following:

We invite Rhea, Therasia, Posidaeja, [AND OTHER DEITY NAMES IF APPROPRIATE] to join us in this sacred rite.

Then move on to the Welcoming.

Welcoming
In this section the people welcome each other while they also welcome the deities into the temple. In a sense, we're also welcoming the temple itself into being for the timespan of the ritual. Move into the ritual space in an orderly procession while singing the Welcoming Chant. As a reminder, the tunes to all

the chants are in the Ariadne's Tribe playlist on my YouTube channel.

We enter the temple in love and peace;
We enter the temple together.

Repeat the chant at least three times, until everyone is inside the ritual area. If it's a group ritual and there are both clergy and other participants present, the clergy should gather near the altar. Everyone else should position themselves where they can see the altar area.

Now the people who carried the deity figurines into the ritual should place them on the altar. Do this one at a time, with the Mothers going first in their usual order (Rhea, Therasia, Posidaeja). Once each person has set their figurine on the altar, they should place the basket or tray and the cover on the side table. Then the next person takes their turn.

When we welcome the deities, we acknowledge that their presence creates the temple for the duration of the ritual. This heightens our relationship with them, which is an aspect of ritual we treasure. Once all the figurines have been placed on the altar, we welcome the Mothers with a call and response:

Leader: *Rhea is here!*
Participants: *We are children of the Earth!*
Leader: *Therasia is here!*
Participants: *We are children of the Sun!*
Leader: *Posidaeja is here!*
Participants: *We are children of the Sea!*

For rituals that involve "starry" deities like Minos, Antheia, or Tauros Asterion, we also welcome Ourania, our Star Mother, in this part of the rite. In those cases, we add these two lines at the end of the Welcoming:

Leader: *Ourania is here!*
Participants: *We are children of the Stars!*

Once we've acknowledged the Mothers' presence, we formally welcome all the deities we've invited to the ritual:

Welcome, Rhea! Welcome, Therasia! Welcome, Posidaeja! Welcome [OTHER DEITY NAMES]! The temple is consecrated by your presence.

Offering

This part of the ritual is our chance to show that we don't want to take without first giving. We're in a two-way relationship with the deities, just like with our human friends and family. Making offerings helps to weave us more deeply into our relationship with the divine. After all, the deities aren't cosmic vending machines. When we treat them like honored guests and respected elders, they show us an equal measure of generosity and respect. I'll share more details about what kinds of items and substances we use for offerings and how we dispose of them after the ritual is over, further down in this chapter.

Before we make the offering, we state the purpose of the ritual in clear, concise language:

We have come here today to [CELEBRATE, ASK FOR HELP, GIVE THANKS, ETC.].

We usually make an offering to the deity or deities who are the focus of the ritual, the ones whose figurines now sit on the altar. It's OK to also make an offering to the Three Mothers, even if they aren't the main deities in the ritual, and even if you don't have figurines for them on the altar. To make the offering, first retrieve the offering item(s) from the side table and move in front of the altar. Then present the offering for each deity individually. Begin each offering by saying the following:

Today we offer [OFFERING ITEM(S)] to [DEITY].

Then set the item(s) on the altar or pour the libation. Be sure to put any empty containers back on the side table; don't leave them on the altar. If a clergy person is embodying the deity you're giving the offering to, they can respond with the following words if they feel called to do so:

I have received your offering, and I thank you for it.

Go through this process (announce the offering, place it on the altar, and allow the person embodying the deity to respond if they wish) for each of the offerings, if there's more than one, before moving on. After all the offerings have been given, it's time to sing the Offering Chant, repeating it in full three times:

We give, we share, we return to you
From all that we have received
We offer our bounty in thankfulness
In joy we shall proceed

Allow a few moments for the energy of the chant to die down and for the participants to contemplate the gifts they've given to the deities before moving on to the next part of the ritual.

Listening
Now that we've offered our gifts to the deities, it's our turn to receive. So we can hear what the deities have to say to us, it's time to stop talking and listen instead. This "sacred listening" can take many different forms: a guided meditation, a mystery play, divination, walking a labyrinth, any activity that expresses

the purpose of your ritual. This part of the ritual can also include Confluence, which I'll explain in detail further down in this chapter. This is your chance to be creative and choose an activity or method that helps the participants experience the main concept behind the ritual.

Regardless of the form the Listening part of the ritual takes, be sure to keep your senses open for any messages the deities have to share with you. You should also be aware that sometimes, deities besides the ones you officially invited into the ritual will "pop in" to help. Be open to hearing what they have to share as well. It's a good idea to end this section with a few moments of silence before moving on to the Returning, to let everyone find their focus again.

Returning

In this final portion of the ritual, we *return* thanks to the deities for their presence, and we *return* to the Big World as we complete the ritual and have a procession out of the sacred space, carrying the gift of our experiences with us. We begin the Returning with a call and response that's similar to the one in the Welcoming section.

Leader: *Rhea is with us!*
Participants: *We thank the Earth Mother!*
Leader: *Therasia is with us!*
Participants: *We thank the Sun Mother!*
Leader: *Posidaeja is with us!*
Participants: *We thank the Sea Mother!*

If the Welcoming included a call and response with Ourania, the Returning should include one as well:

Leader: *Ourania is with us!*
Participants: *We thank the Star Mother!*

Then we offer our thanks to all the deities we invited into the ritual:

We thank the Mothers! We thank [OTHER DEITY NAMES]!
Blessings upon you all, now and forever!

Now it's time for the people who carried the deity figurines into the ritual space to retrieve them from the altar. Do this in the opposite order from the way you put them on the altar (last in, first out). One at a time, take the basket or tray and the cover from the side table, then go to the altar and place the deity figurine in the basket or on the tray. Don't cover it yet. Wait near the altar until all the figurines are done.

Once all the deity figurines have been removed from the altar, everyone should line up for the Returning procession. Use the same order you were in when you entered the ritual space, and take a few moments to quiet down and focus again. When everyone is lined up, focused, and ready to complete the ritual, process out of the area while singing the Returning Chant:

We carry the temple's blessings out into the world;
Peace be on us all, peace be on us all, peace be on us all.

Sing the chant at least three times, even if it doesn't take that long for everyone to move out of the ritual space. If it takes longer, keep singing until everyone has left the ritual space.

Finally, sound the musical instrument three times (the same instrument you used to begin the ritual) and cover all the deity figurines.

Finishing Up

The rite is ended, but the process isn't over until you've disassembled the altar and cleaned up. As a reminder, we don't discuss our experiences in the ritual until we're finished cleaning up. This lets the experience have some space, and it gives the energy some time to settle. Cleanup is as much of a group experience as the ritual itself, so if this was a group ritual, everyone should pitch in however they can.

First, dispose of any offerings respectfully and responsibly. I've detailed the best options in the section about offerings at the end of this chapter. Be sure to consider how you're going to dispose of your offerings when you're planning the ritual, so you can organize that part ahead of time and won't be rushed or have trouble once the ritual is over.

Next, disassemble the altar. If you're somewhere like a public park, simply pack up the altar ware so it's ready to take home. Otherwise, put the ritual items away, including any decorations and other objects you might have used. Don't rush this part. Be as respectful and mindful as you were when you set up for the ritual. Everyone should participate as they're able so the cleanup goes quickly without having to hurry.

Once you've cleaned up from the ritual, it's time to share food and good company. It's nice to share a meal after a group ritual, in keeping with the tradition of communal feasting that went on for many centuries in Minoan Crete. Eating together and discussing your experiences during the ritual is a great way to complete the process, ground and center, and begin carrying the blessings of the rite out into the world.

The Rite of Confluence

The second type of ritual I want to share with you here is one we call Confluence. This rite helps us sync up with the universe that we're an intricate part of, and it reminds us there's a spark of the divine within each of us and in the world around us. It's not just about connection, but about allowing ourselves and our lives to change form as they need to. And it's a reminder that every interaction we have, with other humans, with deities, and with other inspired beings, changes us.

Confluence is symbolized by pouring two streams of liquid together, out of two separate containers and into a third container. This pouring of water is always accompanied by three sacred questions and other specific words and acts. If you leave any of them out, you're not performing Confluence. Confluence is the full ritual, not just the pouring-together of the water. Confluence can be a part of any ritual, in the Listening section, as long as its symbology is appropriate to the meaning and purpose of the ceremony. It can also be performed separately, as a ritual in its own right.

Confluence encompasses the idea of communion with deity as well as connection with other humans and with the non-human beings whose spirits also fill our world. This ritual is fully inclusive and doesn't reference gender at all, though some people have compared it to the Wiccan Great Rite. Confluence can be used in similar ways to the Great Rite, but its symbolism is broader and includes more possibilities.

The website Dictionary.com offers the following five definitions for *confluence*:

1. a flowing together of two or more streams, rivers, or the like.
2. their place of junction.
3. a body of water formed by the flowing together of two or more streams, rivers, or the like.
4. a coming together of people or things; concourse.
5. a crowd or throng; assemblage.

So the word *confluence* means "flowing together," which is, of course, what happens with the water, but there's more to it than that. Confluence is also the place where the flowing-together happens as well as the new being created by the flowing-together, whether it's two rivers becoming a third new body of water, individuals becoming a cohesive group gathered for sacred purposes, two people becoming a married couple, or any of a myriad other ways confluence can occur.

Part of the meaning and symbolism of Confluence is that we're irretrievably changed by our interactions with others; and here, *others* includes humans, deities, spirit allies, non-human animals, nature spirits, and other kinds of beings. Our connections with others alter us in profound ways, and Confluence represents both the connection and the change, both communion and creation. Every instance of Confluence results in something new coming into the world.

When we perform Confluence, we connect with the goddess Kalaeja. You read about her earlier, in the chapter about the deities. We're all alive in Kalaeja's dance, flowing together with her and with each other. This is what we celebrate with Confluence.

The physical process of performing Confluence looks deceptively simple. We pour two streams of water together so they become a single stream. Once you've poured them together, you can't separate out the original streams. Sure, you can divide the water in two and pour two streams from it again, but the two new streams won't contain exactly the same molecules as the original two. The process of mixing produces irrevocable change in the water. That's the key. We're changed by our interactions with each other, the inspirited world around us, and the divine in ways that can't be undone and in ways that often aren't easily visible.

As with any ritual, your focus and mindfulness are an important part of the process. Just pouring water together doesn't create Confluence. What does create it is attentively and thoughtfully pouring the water while also performing the other parts of the rite. As I mentioned before, if you don't complete the other acts, it isn't Confluence.

You can perform Confluence as a stand-alone ritual, without using the ritual format I described in the first part of this chapter and without doing anything else to accompany it. You could do this, for instance, as a self-healing rite to "pour yourself back together." Or you can include it in the Listening portion of any larger ritual. Either way, Confluence can be either a solitary or a group ritual. If it's solitary, you'll need to say all the parts out loud and take all the actions yourself. Don't leave anything out.

Because the water that's used in this ritual is special and is also changed by Confluence, you can't just dump it out afterward. Please note there's a particular way to dispose of it, and be sure to make allowances for this when you're planning your ritual. Here's how to perform Confluence:

The Preparation
One person will lead the rite. If you're doing it solitary, obviously this will be you. The leader must wear the color red in some form so it's visible to the participants, preferably on their head, hands, heart, or all three. This could be red jewelry, makeup, henna, a hat or scarf or hair ornament, clothing, or even a tattoo with red elements in it. It needs to be the literal color red, not the figurative reddish-orange color of ginger hair. Though if your hair, or a portion of it, is dyed a true red color, that will work!

You'll need two pitchers with equal amounts of water in them, plus a bowl to pour the water into. The bowl needs to be big enough to hold all the water without spilling. The pitchers don't have to be identical, but if you can, choose pitchers and a bowl whose color and design underscore the meaning and purpose of the ritual. If you're performing Confluence as part of a larger ritual, the pitchers and bowl can begin on the side table, or you can put them on the altar when you set up for the rite.

The Opening and the Three Questions

The leader begins the ritual by saying "Kalaeja is with us!" While they're saying it, they lay their palm on their chest, above their heart, then reach their hand out, palm upward, toward the other participants. If you're performing this ritual as a solitary, simply reach your hand out in front of you.

Now the leader asks the Three Questions. If you're doing this alone, you'll still need to ask the questions, and answer them, out loud.

1. *Who wishes to pour themselves together?*
2. *Why do you wish to do so?*
3. *How long do you wish to stay blended?*

The other participants must answer the Three Questions out loud. If you're performing Confluence as part of a larger ritual, you can offer the participants a prefab answer to make things easier. For a wedding, you could ask each question twice, once to the couple who will do the actual pouring of the water, and a second time to the gathered family and friends, since the answers will be different for the two groups.

For instance, after asking Question 1, you could say, "If you wish to pour yourself together with the others in this ritual, please answer this question by saying 'I do.'" Or for Question 2, you could ask the question and then say, "If you wish to do so in order to share in the sacred experience of this celebration, please answer this question by saying 'I do.'"

Question 3 is especially important because in a way, Confluence is like a light switch. You can set a timer so it goes off automatically at a certain point. An example of this would be a couple who's getting married answering Question 3 with "so long as love shall last." Or, like a light switch, you can turn it off manually. This is a good choice if you're including Confluence as a way for people to connect during a ritual but you want to release that energy at the end of the rite. In that case, you would end Confluence at the end of the Listening section of the ritual using the wording described below in "The Ending." Regardless of which way you choose, you have to specify when Confluence ends when you answer Question 3.

The Confluence

Once the Three Questions have been asked and answered, it's time to mingle the waters. If the pitchers and bowl are on the side table, now is the time to move them to the altar. If you're performing Confluence as a solitary, you'll pick up both pitchers yourself, one in each hand. But if this is a group ritual, two people should do the pouring, with each one picking up one pitcher.

Hold the pitchers steady a short distance above the bowl. Then pour the two waters together slowly, allowing the two streams to dance together into one as they pour down into the bowl. Take your time, so everyone has the opportunity to observe the waters mingling. Continue slowly until all the water is in the bowl, then set the empty pitchers down on either side of the bowl and continue with the rest of your ritual. If you're performing Confluence as a stand-alone rite, simply end it now as I've described below.

The Ending

If you want the Confluence to end when your ritual ends, then do that at the end of the Listening section, before the Returning completes the rite. You can also end it shortly after performing it, if you'd like to move on to another part of your ritual. If you're performing Confluence by itself, then end it whenever you're ready, perhaps after some meditation and contemplation.

To end Confluence, the leader says:

With gratitude we acknowledge the gift of Confluence. The Confluence ends now, but we are changed by it. For a few moments, we wait in silence to make space for who we have become through pouring ourselves together.

The Wrap-Up

Once your ritual is over, you're left with a bowl of water. Be sure to plan ahead for this aspect of the rite. The important thing is that the water has to be left undisturbed in the bowl until it all evaporates. Don't pour it into another container, and don't set it where an animal can drink out of it or where it's likely to be disturbed.

Don't panic! You can move it if you need to. Maybe you did your ritual at a local park and you need to carry everything home afterward. In a case like that, cover the bowl securely and take it wherever you need to. When you get home, set it someplace safe, uncover it, and let it evaporate. Since you need to leave the water to evaporate, you might consider using a smaller rather than larger amount of water for Confluence in the first place. Unless, of course, you have a place where a large bowl of water can sit undisturbed for an extended period of time.

Dissolution

What if you performed Confluence and answered the questions in a way that had it last a long time, and now you want it to stop before it "runs out" based on the answer you gave? Don't worry, there's a way to do that. This might happen, for instance, if you use Confluence during a wedding ceremony and the couple eventually separate.

This method of "manually turning off the switch" is called Dissolution. You can use it at any point after you perform Confluence, and you don't need any of the items (the pitchers or the bowl) you originally used. Simply make yourself a water mirror, which is a round container, such as a bowl, full of still water. Wait until the water is absolutely still, then look at your reflection in the water. While you're gazing at your reflection, tap the center of the water so the image is dispersed in the ripples, then immediately look away from the water. Don't look back at the water in any way that will give you a clear reflection. Dispose of the water as soon as possible by pouring it down a drain, or if a drain isn't available, then into a hole in the ground. This is one rare instance in Tribe ritual when pouring a ritual substance down a drain is the preferred choice.

Making Offerings

The Minoans were fond of making offerings to their deities in great abundance, as the archaeological remains indicate. So we take inspiration from them in our modern spiritual practice. Making an offering is a way to show your appreciation and gratitude for the divine in your life. It's a way to demonstrate your devotion and affection. Offerings connect us with the Minoans and our ancient ancestors who used this activity as a way to maintain and reinforce their relationships with the deities.

Most of the time, we make offerings to one specific deity, or perhaps a small group of them. But it's also possible to make offerings to the entire Minoan pantheon in general. How you frame an offering, and which deity or deities you give it to, will depend on your intention for making the offering in the first place. Offerings are always included as part of our formal ritual structure, which you read about earlier in this chapter. But you can also make offerings outside of ritual, by themselves, as a stand-alone sacred act. That's actually the most common way many us make offerings, because it's an easy way to interact with deity and make the all-important connection with the divine without taking too much time out of a busy schedule.

I discussed earlier what tangible ancient Minoan offerings looked like. Modern ones are often similar: food, drink, flowers, incense. Solid items like bread and fruit can go directly on the altar or on an offering stand that is itself placed on the altar. Modern footed cake plates are remarkably similar to Minoan offering stands, so they're a popular choice. If you're making the offering outside, you can set up a makeshift altar or simply leave the offering in an appropriate spot.

If you're making a libation (a liquid offering), your best bet is to pour it into a container on the altar. Poured offerings appear to have been a major aspect of Minoan religion, judging from the hundreds of rhytons that have been found at archaeological sites and the images on Minoan seals. But just setting a cup of a liquid on the altar isn't necessarily the best choice. The act of pouring had meaning in Minoan religion, so we make the effort to pour liquid offerings instead of just setting them out. If you're making a libation outside, you can pour it directly onto the ground. If the offering is intended for Underworld deities, you could even dig a hole in the ground to pour it into. This is reminiscent of the "moats" around the square pillars in the lower levels of Minoan temples, where liquid offerings may have been poured as a way to send them to the Underworld.

If you make an offering of incense, when you're done, all that's left is some ash to clean up. And if you pour some wine onto the ground outdoors, there's nothing left afterward. But in many other cases, there's some food or drink or other perishable item like fresh flowers still on the altar. What should you do with those leftovers, and when?

First, let me say, we don't know for certain what the Minoans did with the remains of perishable offerings. We know they made these sorts of offerings, but we have to decide for ourselves how to deal with those remains in our modern spiritual practice. We've developed some basic traditions regarding how to deal with cleaning up offerings, especially perishable ones.

When we make the offering, we leave the item on the altar for however long feels right to us: a few hours, overnight, a set number of days, until the next full moon, or some other span of time. This choice should take into account the perishability of the item as well as any intuitive messages you might receive from the deity or deities you've given the offering to. Milk will spoil quickly, for instance, so leaving it out for long isn't a good idea. But the worst that's likely to happen to fresh flowers is they'll wilt, so they can stay a while.

In general, food offerings should be removed from the altar before they spoil. If you have access to a compost pile, that's the most respectful way to dispose of food offerings. Fresh flowers can be set outdoors to return to the earth. But food offerings should be disposed of in a way that protects wildlife from eating them, since many human foods can harm wild animals. If you don't have access to a compost pile, food offering remains can be placed in the trash. But the compost is preferable if it's available.

Liquid offerings poured outdoors disappear into the ground. But if you've poured an offering into a container, you'll need to dispose of it afterward. The preferred choice is always to pour it onto the ground outdoors, in a location where any insects it attracts won't cause problems. If that's not possible, you can pour it down a drain. But outdoors is always preferable.

Let me say here that we rarely offer large amounts of food or drink at any one time. The typical offering size is what you might call a generous single serving size: a thick slice of freshly-made bread, a full cup of wine, a perfect piece of fruit. If you're dedicating an entire meal to sacred purposes, such as a dining rite to honor the ancestors, your offering should be a small portion of the food served on its own plate specifically for the ancestors and/or the deities. The rest of the meal is for the humans.

In the Tribe, we don't practice reversion of offerings. This method was popular in ancient Egypt, where people gave enormous amounts of food to the deities via the temples. The food was left in the temples long enough for the deities to imbibe the spirit of the offering, then it was removed and used to feed the temple clergy. These days, we don't have temples full of clergy who need to be fed. So we make small food offerings and dispose of them respectfully afterward.

There's another type of offering I'd like to talk about here, an intangible type, an activity dedicated to a deity as an offering. This can be a helpful task like cleaning up a park or working at a soup kitchen, or a personal endeavor like running a footrace or learning a new dance. Although we have no direct evidence the Minoans made these kinds of offerings, they're extensively documented as common in the ancient world. So it's likely the Minoans did something similar.

The next question is, what kinds of offerings does each deity prefer? We don't have any clear evidence of specifics from Minoan times, so we've had to listen to the deities in our modern spiritual practice and work out the details that way. I'll share some possibilities below, but I also encourage you to listen to the deities yourself via meditation, prayer, or journeywork and find out what kinds of offerings they might prefer from you. You can also set a proposed offering near the altar, not directly on it, and ask the deity if it's acceptable. Then pay attention to your senses. Do you feel compelled to go ahead and put the offering on the altar? Or do you feel a little uncomfortable, like maybe you should remove it from the area?

If you'd like to start with some offerings we've already learned the deities like, I've listed some possibilities below. These are items you can be sure they'll be happy with under the vast majority of circumstances. So here are the "safe bets" for the Minoan deities, as well as some offering types that you can experiment with to see if they work for you. Let's begin with the Mothers.

Rhea: Milk is always a safe bet with Rhea. Animal milk (cow, goat, sheep) and most kinds of non-dairy milk will work, though she doesn't like coconut milk much, we've found. Honey is also always a safe bet. She enjoys the kinds of fruits that grew in ancient Crete: figs, dates, grapes, and quinces, either fresh or dried. Grain offerings also work well for her. Rhea is the Grain-Mother, after all. She seems to prefer cooked grain in forms like bread or porridge, but heads and stalks of dried grain are also acceptable; extra points if you grew it yourself. The Minoans had three kinds of wheat plus barley and rye, so those are your best choices. Rhea also enjoys offerings of wool, especially unspun and otherwise unprocessed (unscoured, for those of you who are into the fiber arts). If you can get some fresh fleece from a farmer or a spinning and weaving supply shop, that's your best choice. Some people can offer her white wine, but she doesn't always like it, so check with her first.

Therasia: As you might expect, fire offerings please our Sun-Mother. She prefers oil lamps to candles, though she will accept candle offerings, and she especially likes those wood wick candles that crackle like a fire. But she *really* likes an actual fire: campfire, bonfire, fire in your fireplace, little fire in your cauldron, however you can manage it (always taking appropriate safety precautions, of course!). She also likes fiery incense like frankincense. Some of us like to offer "hot" incense like cinnamon and ginger, which were unknown to the Minoans but which fit the bill in the modern world; she seems to like them. Beware, though, she isn't fond of hot peppers. She happily receives offerings of dates and quinces, the two fruits associated with her, as well as olive leaves (but not the fruit, which belongs to Korydallos). Saffron is sacred to her, so offerings of saffron threads are a good, though expensive, choice. You can also offer saffron dissolved in white wine, in a clear container so the deep golden color the saffron dyes the liquid is visible. Therasia also likes retsina, the stronger the better, and she's the only Minoan deity who appears to enjoy distilled liquor, preferably amber in color (dark rum, whiskey, Scotch, that sort of thing).

Posidaeja: The best offering for Grandmother Ocean is water from any natural source. It doesn't have to be sea-water, since ultimately she's the Mother of all the Waters, not just the ocean. Avoid chemical-treated tap water if you can; bottled spring water is OK, as is well water. She also enjoys fresh flowers and seashells. Putting flowers on the altar is always acceptable, but if you have the chance, making a flower wreath or garland and tossing it into the ocean or some other body of water is a marvelous offering. Please use the daisy chain method whenever possible to make wreaths and garlands for her. If you must include strings or ribbons, make sure they're fully biodegradable and made of non-toxic materials.

Serpent Mother: She enjoys offerings of pure (not chemically treated) water, wine, and whole uncooked grains. She also likes incense whose main ingredient is resin. The Minoans had myrrh, frankincense, terebinth, copal, and labdanum, so these are the best choices. Avoid synthetically scented incense. As a deity who works to create healing change in the world, the Serpent Mother enjoys offerings of labor, especially volunteer work whose purpose is healing and renewal. This might involve something like soup kitchens or HIV awareness. Since this kind of offering is a big commitment, it's best to check with the goddess first to be sure she's happy with your specific choice before you dive into the actual work.

Ourania: Her preferred offering is pure water from a natural source (it doesn't have to be drinkable), with the offering made outside at night underneath the stars. Ideally, you would pour the water into a black or dark-colored bowl, preferably made of stone. Regardless of the type of bowl you use, set the water out so the stars reflect in it for a little while before offering it. But don't pour it out to make the offering. Simply put the bowl in an appropriate spot and leave it until dawn, at which point you can dispose of it.

Those are the kinds of offerings the Mothers enjoy. Now let's find out what their children like.

Amalthea: Goat's milk and honey are her preferred offerings. Like Rhea, she accepts offerings of wool. If you can get mohair or other goat hair, that's even better. She also enjoys fresh goat cheese as an offering; it's similar to the kinds of fresh cheeses the Minoans made. Stick with plain cheese, though, since many of the added flavorings, such as cranberries and tomatoes, are from the Americas and tend to confuse her. She will accept red wine as an offering, but she prefers goat's milk, goat cheese, and honey. If you want to offer incense to her, choose one that's heavy on labdanum, a resin traditionally gathered from the beards of goats that browsed on the shrubs it comes from.

Antheia: Her favorite offering is fresh flowers, especially ones in shades of yellow or gold and white. She loves bouquets, vases full of flowers, garlands, and flower necklaces and crowns. If you can get them, she loves fresh duck and goose eggs, preferably whole and uncooked. Myrtle (Myrtus communis) is sacred to her, so she likes offerings of the fresh berries and leafy stems as well as myrtle liqueur (Mirto). She also enjoys offerings of white and rosé wine.

Arachne: Our weaver-of-fate goddess enjoys offerings of very dark red wine and fiber arts activities and products. If you spin, for instance, you could make yarn and give some of it to her. You can also offer your labor in making a fiber arts project such as a crocheted or knitted blanket and then donate the finished item to people in need, such as a shelter or hospital.

Ariadne: Since Ariadne has two faces, one in the Underworld and one in the World Above, there are two categories of offerings for her. For her World Above face, she enjoys white wine, white lilies, saffron, and sprouted wheat. For her aspect as Queen of the Dead, she likes pomegranates (the whole fruit, arils, or juice), poppyseeds, red lilies, and red wine. You can offer honey to either of her aspects.

Asclepius: This healer-god, son of Hygeia, enjoys honey as an offering. It's not just tasty; it also had many medicinal uses in the ancient world. He also accepts offerings of fresh Mediterranean herbs that have medicinal properties, such as lavender, sage, and rosemary.

Britomartis: She accepts offerings of dark red wine. Her wildness also means she enjoys offerings of wild land, perhaps a corner of your yard that you choose not to mow or cultivate but simply let grow as it will. If you dedicate a bit of land to her in this way, it's a good place to pour out wine offerings to her. She also enjoys offerings of outdoor physical activity like hiking to a special place in nature.

Daedalus: He enjoys having an oil lamp, not a candle, lit for him as an offering. He also accepts offerings of olive oil and castor oil, but food in general isn't a good choice for him. Since he's the inventor/smith god, you can dedicate those kinds of activities to him as offerings.

Dionysus: The God of Ecstasy loves libations of wine, beer, and mead. He doesn't generally care for hard liquor, though, and he reacts unpredictably to wine and beer flavored with herbs, fruit, and other substances, so check first before offering these. Interestingly, he'll also accept offerings of homemade red wine vinegar, but not usually the store-bought stuff unless it has a "mother" (vinegar culture) in it.

Eileithyia: Honey and poppyseed are the traditional offerings to our midwife-goddess who is also the Underworld face of our sun goddess Therasia. But she also enjoys milk of all sorts (animal or plant) and fresh-baked bread, especially if it's still warm from the oven. Spread a little honey on it before offering it for the best demonstration of your affection for her.

Europa: Her preferred offerings are whole cow's milk and wine, separately or in combination. She accepts both red and white wine, so think carefully about the symbolism of the color in relation to the purpose of your offering before choosing.

Hygeia: This healer-goddess, who is a face of our sun goddess Therasia, particularly enjoys white wine with honey and saffron mixed in it. She also likes incense that has a warm, sunny aroma.

Kaulo: Since Kaulo's domain is the expression of joy through the human body, that sort of activity is the best offering for him. How can you show joy with your body? Dancing is one possibility, and you don't have to be formal or fancy about it as long as you're having fun. Another option is simply to move around in any way that feels good to you. A simple, quick offering could be blowing him kisses at the altar.

Korydallos: He enjoys receiving offerings of brightly colored flowers, sweet-smelling incense, honey, olives, sweet wine, and

117

mead. He also likes homemade bread, still warm from the oven, preferably slathered with butter and honey. He also appreciates acts of kindness, particularly those toward our fellow human beings. So if you want to do some volunteer work and dedicate it to him as an offering, consider helping out at someplace like a nursing home, a homeless shelter, or a center for disadvantaged youth.

Melissae: As you might expect, these bee-spirit goddesses enjoy offerings of honey, mead, and honey ale. At harvest time you can offer cooked grain products such as bread or porridge, preferably drizzled with honey. The Melissae also really like beeswax candles, even though the Minoans didn't have candles, only oil lamps. The more your beeswax candles smell like honey, the more the Melissae will like them.

Minelathos: He likes libations of the darkest of red wines. Like his counterpart Britomartis, he also appreciates having land left wild in his honor. This could be as simple as a corner of your yard or as major as an entire property being rewilded. If you dedicate wild land to him, it's an excellent place to pour out libations in his honor.

Minocapros: He enjoys offerings of red wine, the darker the better. He also likes incense that's heavy on the labdanum, the resin that was traditionally gathered from the beards of goats that browsed on the shrubs that produce it.

Minos: He enjoys offerings of pure, fresh water, preferably from a natural source such as a well or a lake, river, or stream. Bottled spring water also works here if it's your only option. To make your offering extra special, pour the water into a bowl, preferably a dark-colored one, and leave it out in the light of the full moon for a little while before setting it on the altar. Do be aware that he doesn't much care for wine.

Minotaur: Red wine is the usual offering for the beloved Moon-Bull. He's especially fond of the kind of dark red wine that's often called "bull's blood."

Potnia Chromaton: The Lady of the Colors enjoys brightly colored offerings: flowers, fruit juice, fresh fruit, even items like ribbons in bright colors. She also likes any kind of offering that you've dyed or painted yourself. So you could offer her a small painting that you made, or some dyed fabric or yarn. If you'll be using a cup, bowl, or offering stand, it should also be brightly colored, preferably in multiple different colors.

Talos: The Bronze One enjoys offerings that involve metal, preferably bronze or copper, at least in color, if not in actual material. So you could pour him some water in a bronze cup or bowl. Or offer him a small metal gadget of some sort; he's quite fond of those metal brain teaser puzzle toys that come in shapes like two keys that you have to figure out how to take apart or a box that you have to figure out how to open.

Tauros Asterion: He enjoys libations of dark red wine and ruby port. The kind of red wine called "bull's blood" is a good choice. He also likes having physical labor dedicated to him as an offering, especially any earthy activity like digging ditches, planting trees, or cleaning the litter from a local park or roadside. If you're likely to sweat and feel your muscles working while you're doing it, he'll probably enjoy it as an offering.

Thaena, Sydaili, and Eshuumna: These unusual deities prefer an unusual kind of offering: light. The best offering for the

Unseen Rainbow (all three of these deities together) is a visible rainbow; not a rainbow flag or other painted design, and not even a photo of an actual rainbow in the sky, but a real rainbow. How to do that? Simply hang one of those cut-glass suncatchers where the light shines on it so it throws a rainbow right onto your altar or some other spot that you'd like to dedicate to them.

Thumia: Since Thumia's domain is the expression of joy through the human body, that sort of activity is the best offering for her. In particular, Thumia enjoys offerings that involve vocalization. Singing, chanting, and humming are good choices. You could also offer an out-loud reading of joyous poetry, prose, or a portion of a play. And as with Kaulo, a delightful quick offering involves blowing kisses to her at the altar.

Zagreus: The Bull Who Comes Wreathed in Flowers in the Blooming Time prefers fresh flowers as an offering. Any color will do, but a variety of different colors is best. He also enjoys floral-scented incense, white wine, and the kinds of whole grains (wheat berries and barley groats) the Minoans harvested as the Blooming Time began and that cattle like to eat.

I've just shared a lot of offering types the Minoan deities enjoy. But there are some they're not so keen on, and some that can provoke strong negative reactions. For instance, our experience suggests it's not a good idea to offer meat, not even to the Horned Ones. Now, there have been a few people who hunted and offered a small portion of their venison to the Minelathos or Britomartis and had it accepted. But those are unusual circumstances. Purchased meat is likely to result in a disgruntled, if not angry, deity. The only exception to this is if there is meat involved as part of the meal in a dining ritual, and you're serving the entire meal to the deity. In this case, they don't generally seem to mind. But it's still a good idea to check first, either with meditation and prayer or by setting the offering near the altar and waiting for the deity's response.

Another item to avoid offering is blood. Blood of any sort (venous blood, menstrual blood, birthing blood, the blood from an animal you've hunted or slaughtered) has powerful connotations. Its presence in a sacred setting can easily offend or anger the deities. Offering your own blood can also tie you to the deity in ways you may not intend. Be especially careful when offering blood of any sort to Underworld deities unless that's where you want to end up. If, in spite of this warning, you feel compelled to offer blood of any sort, please take the time to connect with the deity and make sure you understand the implications of what you're doing. The deities' reactions will tend to differ from one worshiper to another, so you can't necessarily depend on someone else's experience here. Even with all that said, I don't recommend it.

We know from the art that the Minoans collected and used the blood of sacrificed animals in their religion, but there were doubtless strong rules and taboos associated with the practice. There were probably women's rituals involving menstrual blood, but we aren't sure exactly what was involved or what the protocol was. In both cases, well-trained professional clergy would have overseen these activities. Since we don't know for certain how the Minoans managed any of these rites, it's best to tread very carefully and avoid offering blood of any sort.

In general, though, you don't need to panic about offerings. Start with the ones I've listed above, then expand as you feel comfortable by listening to the deities. Your relationship with them is unique, so the kinds of offerings they might like from you could vary a little from what I've discussed. The most important thing is that you make offerings and put your energy into your connection with the deities.

Offerings are a fairly common part of modern Pagan spiritual practice, regardless of tradition. So, too, is magic, though it can look quite different from one tradition to another. What might magic have looked like in ancient Minoan times, and how can it play a part in modern Minoan spiritual practice? We'll explore those possibilities in the next chapter.

Chapter 6

Making Magic and Living the Spiritual Life

Did the Minoans perform magic? Yes, just as their neighbors in Egypt, Mesopotamia, and the Levant did. It was a common practice in the Bronze Age Mediterranean. Like everyone around them, the Minoans called on their deities to aid them in achieving their desires and goals. We actually have some evidence of Minoan magic in written form.

The London Medical Papyrus, written in about 1600 BCE, was found in Egypt and is now housed in the British Museum (hence the "London" in the name). So it's from the era when the Minoans were at their height, right before the Thera eruption. This document contains dozens of magical incantations. Almost half of them are healing magic, performed as remedies to treat medical conditions like eye diseases and burns.

The papyrus is a collection of incantations from Egypt and surrounding regions, including the Levant, Nubia, and Crete. Two of the medical entries have been identified as Minoan because they're described as "Keftiu" in the language of ancient Egypt. As I mentioned earlier, Keftiu is the word the Egyptians used to describe the people of ancient Crete. The incantations on the papyrus aren't in the Egyptian language, though. They're Minoan which has been transliterated, in other words, written out sound for sound, in the Egyptian script.

Since we don't yet understand the Minoan language (Linear A hasn't been deciphered), these incantations are difficult to translate, even though we know roughly what they sounded like because we can read the Egyptian script they were recorded in. But scholars have identified deity names within them. So we can say with confidence the Minoans used magic in much the same way many other cultures of the time did, by using incantations (spoken magical formulas) to call on their deities for help with specific problems.

Divination is another kind of magic that was probably popular among the Minoans, since it was common among their neighboring eastern Mediterranean cultures. Auguries of all sorts are likely, from the flight of birds or the arrangement of animal entrails to scrying, perhaps in water or wine or the polished bronze mirrors the Minoans used. Again, it's likely they performed these acts with the aid of their deities.

Magic is one of the aspects of Paganism that excites a lot of modern people. Often, we perform magic to attract good fortune, either in material form (income, job prospects) or in relational form (romance, love, friendship). Protection from the negative aspects of life is also high up on the list of subjects for spell casting. These are all basic human desires, something we modern people have in common with the ancient Minoans.

How does this sort of activity fit in with a deity-focused spiritual practice? It all has to do with your worldview and the way you approach the concept of magic.

Let's start with a basic question: What exactly do we mean by *magic*? In his book *Magick without Tears*, Aleister Crowley famously described magic as "the Science and Art of causing Change to occur in conformity with Will." This definition of magic takes it out of the realm of the divine and the sacred, giving it an air of human domination over nature and the universe.

As I discussed in the chapter about the Minoan worldview, relationship, community, connection and cooperation were hallmarks of Minoan culture and probably also of Minoan religion. An attitude of domination doesn't mesh well with the idea of being respectful of the divine and being a partner with the rest of the world rather than in dominion over it.

So how else might we frame the concept of magic? Thorn Vikaro, a member of Ariadne's Tribe, succinctly describes it as finding "the best way to get from point A to point B," in other words, from where you are now to where you want to be. This includes taking the necessary actions in the material realm as well as allowing the deities to guide us in ritual and spiritual acts. No amount of ritual is likely to get you a new job if you don't send out some resumes and fill in some applications.

The kind of magic I mentioned above in Aleister Crowley's definition has an almost combative view of the universe: make your demand, bend the world to your will, and take what you want. To me, Minoan magic is more like: figure out which stream will take you where you want to go and get in it, swimming with the current so it powers you.

Since the "ordering the universe around" style of magic doesn't fit with the way we think the Minoans understood the world, we choose to perform deity-led magic instead. That is, magic is just one part of our relationship with the deities. They help us with it, as they do with so many other things.

Part of the "swimming with the current" aspect is that we humans are limited in our ability to view and understand the greater universe. But the deities have a much greater vantage point than we do. So they can help us along, giving us hints and pointing us in directions we might not otherwise have chosen to go. And the end result may be far more satisfying than we ever expected.

A big part of deity-led magic amounts to working on our personal relationships with the deities then learning to listen to them. Their suggestions can help us get to where we want to go. There aren't right and wrong choices so much as simply the decisions we make and their consequences. The deities can help us understand which decisions to make and what the consequences are likely to be. They teach us not so much how to *do magic* as how to *be magical*.

But magic is only one aspect of a spiritual life. How does it fit into the bigger picture?

The point of a book like this isn't just to learn about the deities in an academic way. Yes, it's interesting to find out about them, their names and characteristics, what kinds of plants and animals and symbols they're associated with, and so on. But knowing these details is only one step in the process of getting to know them. Once you've found out about the deities and their qualities, the next step is to connect with them in your own life. A relationship with the divine is at the core of the spiritual life.

As I mentioned in the chapter about the Minoan worldview, Bronze Age cultures didn't conceptualize a distinction between the sacred and the mundane the way we do in the industrialized modern West. People back then thought of the divine as permeating all of life. Yes, there were "religious things" they did on specific days, and they spent much of their lives performing what we would call mundane tasks for their livelihoods. But they thought of the deities as moving through the world with them, not "out there" someplace far away or accessible only on specific days or in certain special places. Even the ordinary tasks they undertook to work their jobs and care for their homes and families had a sacred aspect.

How can you incorporate this worldview into your daily activities in a way that adds beauty and meaning to your life? Begin by connecting with the deities.

Some people want a structured spiritual practice that includes altars, shrines, and formal rituals. Others prefer a more casual relationship with the deities, making simple offerings whenever they're inspired to do so and listening to what the deities have to say as they go about their everyday life. There's room for both in a modern Minoan spiritual practice. The important thing to remember is that the deities are at the center of the practice, which can also include your ancestors (those of blood and of spirit) as well. The Minoans appear to have included their own ancestors as a major part of their spiritual practice. Although we don't have communal tombs where we can feast and celebrate our Beloved Dead, we can certainly build altars for them and acknowledge them as an important and sacred aspect of our lives.

I should also note here that the Minoans were a cosmopolitan people, traveling all over the Mediterranean and welcoming foreign visitors to their island's shores. They were familiar with many different pantheons and even borrowed some deities from other cultures. So Minoan spirituality wasn't an exclusive sort of thing in the ancient world. And it doesn't need to be the only aspect of your modern spiritual practice; other pantheons and traditions can round out your experience however you like. The only real rule, if you want to call it that, is to listen to the deities and respect them when you're connecting with them. And we can take inspiration from the Minoans themselves about how to make the connection.

The Minoans practiced their religion in a variety of ways. Many people had home altars, from small and simple to large and elaborate, a practice that will be familiar to modern Pagans. Some larger, wealthier homes included entire shrine rooms, though that was less common. Still, having a "temple room" is a concept many of us are familiar with.

One aspect of Minoan religion that's harder for us to relate to is the presence in ancient Crete of temples, cave shrines, and peak sanctuaries fully staffed with clergy who ran regularly scheduled rituals the public could participate in. The closest we can come to this in the modern world is to gather together in groups and perform rituals together. In Ariadne's Tribe, we do this in local chapters and at Pagan festivals and conferences.

But you don't have to attend a group ritual to connect with the Minoan deities and establish a meaningful spiritual practice. Follow your intuition and your personal preference in deciding how often and how expansively you undertake spiritual activities. Below are some possibilities.

You can connect with the deities one at a time, by making simple offerings to them and listening to what they have to say to you. An offering opens the door to a relationship. It's not a transaction. The deities aren't cosmic vending machines where you put in an offering and out pops a goodie. Making an offering shows you're willing to give before you begin taking. And it makes the deities more positively disposed to interact with you. Although you should know that some of us hear from the deities first and then begin making offerings and performing rituals. That happens, too.

One of my favorite activities to get to know a deity is called "walking with" the deity. You choose a setting and a time during which you invite the deity to walk alongside you, much as you might invite a friend to accompany you on a walk in the park or as you go about your daily activities. This allows you to become accustomed to the deity's energy, and it helps them get to know you as well. It's also good practice in learning to hear what the deity has to share with you.

Bear in mind that, although I use the terms "hear" and "listen" regarding communication with the deities, the information can take many different forms depending on your own psyche and senses. Some people hear actual words in their minds, but many others experience mental images or emotions or physical sensations, and some get "downloads" of concepts without any words attached. However the conversation takes shape, simply allow it to flow and accept the form it takes.

If the Earth itself (herself) is sacred, then we have a greater obligation to take care of it (her). This is one ancient idea we can bring forward into the modern world, to connect with the Earth wherever we happen to be and make the places where we live sacred again. If you like to keep in tune with the cycles of the seasons, you could focus on the myths associated with the festivals in the sacred calendar. Different deities come to the fore at different points in the year. Celebrating the seasonal festivals is a great way to get to know the deities and their mythos.

As I mentioned in the chapter about the sacred calendar, it's all right to move the planting and harvest festivals around to match the seasons in your part of the world. This is a nature religion, so if you don't live in a Mediterranean climate, pay attention to the local cycles where you live and adapt the calendar accordingly.

I'd like to share a couple of sayings we have in Ariadne's Tribe. They might help you get a feeling for the energy behind Minoan spirituality and some ways you can explore more.

The first of these sayings is *reverent joy*. At first this may seem like a contradiction in terms. Many of us have been taught that reverence must be serious, even somber, and largely humorless. But if you look at Minoan art, you can see a kind of sacred joy that permeates it. This is what we experience in Minoan spirituality, in connection with the deities. In other words, reverence doesn't mean being serious, but rather, being attuned to the divine within in and around us, in its many and varied forms. The deities smile and laugh. They exude joy and invite us to share in it as a sacred act.

Of course, there are times when life simply isn't joyful. Days and events when we don't feel like smiling or laughing. The deities are still with us in those times, holding us, holding space for us. But they're also with us when we smile, when we laugh, when we joke and dance and giggle. When we make bad puns and then laughingly groan at them (Korydallos, our punster deity, especially approves). So open yourself to joy, knowing it's every bit as sacred and reverent as anything else you might experience

The second saying builds on the first one: *Together we are joy.* Who is the "we" in this saying? You and me, dear reader, connecting in sacred space via the words in this book. Humans in relationship with each other, holding space for the sacredness in each other's being. And humans in relationship with the deities and all the other non-human beings of this world.

Notice that *relationship* is a major aspect of this description. It's the connection that creates the joy. So the "together" part is just as important as the "joy" part. Everything we do in our spiritual practice is about relationship. It's relationship that weaves its threads through our lives and brings joy.

I hope this book has inspired you to begin a relationship with the Minoan deities, or perhaps to deepen your relationship if you already have a connection with them. They are beautiful, mysterious, and very much alive in the world today. And they delight in connecting with us. I'm very grateful to know them.

Together we are joy.

Glossary

Archaeoastronomy: A type of archeology that studies the astronomy techniques ancient cultures used. This includes the way they arranged their calendars, the use of astronomical alignments in buildings, the star maps they constructed, and the remnants of astronomical information in myth.

Bronze Age: An era in history that ran from about 3300 BCE to about 1200 BCE. It's called the Bronze Age because it's the time when people began the widespread use of bronze for tools, weapons, and decorative items. The Minoans' ancestors settled on Crete thousands of years before the Bronze Age, but their art, architecture, and other aspects of their culture didn't become recognizably Minoan until the Bronze Age.

Comparative mythology: The comparison of myths from different cultures in order to find shared characteristics or to fill in the blanks in the mythology of cultures like the Minoans, whose writing we can't read. Since the Minoans' ancestors were only one of many waves of migration out of Anatolia during the Neolithic era, there were multiple cultures that derived from the same origin and that can offer clues to the content of Minoan myth and religion.

Dance ethnology: The study of traditional dances in their indigenous context, including how they fit into folklore and oral tradition. Many traditional dances have been passed down for generations or even centuries with little change, and even the ones that have changed can still offer clues to the folklore and mythology of earlier times.

Ecstatic posture: A full-body pose used to induce or enhance trance states in ritual. Ecstatic postures have been documented in ancient cultures around the world and are still used today. They can be used by both worshipers and clergy, depending on the purpose of each individual posture. The Minoan salute, in which a worshiper stands upright with the back of their loosely curled fist placed against their forehead, is the most well-known of the ones the Minoans used.

Faience: Also known as Egyptian faience. A type of pottery that's glazed with ground quartz. The Minoans probably learned how to make faience from the Egyptians.

Fresco: A type of painting made by applying plaster to a surface such as a wall then painting directly on the plaster while it's still damp. The paint soaks into the damp plaster, and this helps preserve it.

Gnosis: The personal understanding that an individual has regarding a spiritual subject, gained through their own direct experience. Gnosis usually involves a subject for which we have no available text, artifacts, or other conventional evidence. When a number of different people independently experience the same or very similar gnosis, we call this *shared gnosis*.

Goddess monotheism: The idea that there is only one deity, and that deity is a goddess rather than a god. Sir Arthur Evans thought the Minoans were goddess monotheists who worshiped a single Great Mother Goddess. He was incorrect.

Heliacal rising: Some stars appear and disappear from the sky entirely at various times of the year, not just when they set on a given night. For instance, if you live in the northern hemisphere, you can only see the constellation Orion in the wintertime. The heliacal rising of a star occurs when the star has been invisible for days, weeks, or months. Then one morning it will shine for a few moments just above the eastern horizon, right before the sun rises. After that, it will come into view for a little bit longer each day, but that first appearance is the magical moment of its heliacal rising. The heliacal rising of a star was considered a sign of good fortune in the ancient world, and it still is by modern astrologers.

Heliacal setting: Heliacal setting is, in a sense, the opposite of heliacal rising. When a star or constellation has been visible for a while, over the course of the year it shifts in the sky until eventually it sets in the west just after sunset. The heliacal setting is the last day when the star sets after sunset and the sun is already far enough below the western horizon that the star is visible for a few moments in the evening twilight. After that, the star is no longer visible in the evening.

Larnax: A type of sarcophagus used for secondary burial, once the human remains have decayed until there's nothing left but bones. Minoan larnaxes are rectangular, much smaller than modern coffins, with removable lids. Most of them are ceramic, with painted decorations. But the famous Hagia Triada sarcophagus is made of limestone that has been plastered and painted with frescoes. Toward the end of Minoan times, bathtub-shaped larnaxes came into use. These are ceramic tubs with painted designs on them, also used for secondary burial. No one knows whether these were actual bathtubs that were later reused as larnaxes, or whether they were purpose-made for burial.

Libation: An offering of a liquid such as water or wine, usually poured out (onto the ground or into another container) as part of the ritual process.

Matrilineal culture: A culture in which kinship and descent are traced through the female line. Matrilineal cultures often involve economic and social egalitarianism, sexual freedom, a lack of the concept of illegitimate children, and extended families whose members help each other with child-rearing and economic support.

Merchant marine: A fleet of officially registered ships and boats belonging to a government or civic group. The Minoans may have had an official merchant marine that helped ensure safety for all the ships that sailed to and from Crete. These would likely have been registered to individual cities on

Crete, since the Minoans didn't have a single island-wide government.

Octaeteris: A sacred calendar in which eight solar years, five Venus cycles, and 99 lunations coincide. A lunation is a single moon cycle, from one new moon to the next. Archeoastronomy research tells us the Minoans used the octaeteris along with other sacred calendars.

Pithos: A ceramic storage container, taller than it is wide, with a base that narrows slightly and a top opening about as wide as the whole vessel. The singular is pithos; the plural is pithoi. Minoan pithoi came in a range of sizes, from the smaller ones used as kitchen canisters in private homes to the ones taller than an adult human, used to store grain, wine, and oil in the temples. Pithoi were also used to transport bulk goods via wagon or ship.

Psychopomp: Literally, "soul conductor" or "soul guide." A deity or human spirit worker who helps the spirits of the dead reach the place in the Underworld where they will be at peace. To do this, the deity or spirit worker obviously must have access to the Underworld.

Rhyton: A vessel used to pour liquids as offerings. Rhytons came in multiple different shapes, from plain spouted pitchers to ones shaped like animal heads, whole animals, and elongated animal teats.

Further Reading

A few of these titles may be out of print, but they're all readily available at used booksellers and are well worth searching out. My books are all still in print as of this publication. The titles in this section are my recommendations if you'd like to continue exploring the material you've just read in this book. If you're still hungry for more after reading these, there are more possibilities in the bibliography.

1177 B.C.: The Year Civilization Collapsed by Eric H. Cline. Extensive exploration of the Bronze Age collapse, its possible causes, and regional effects. The Bronze Age collapse began soon after the fall of Knossos and affected the entire eastern Mediterranean and adjacent regions. Its ultimate causes are multiple and complex and probably extend well back into the Minoan era.

Ariadne's Thread: Awakening the Wonders of the Ancient Minoans in Our Modern Lives by Laura Perry, second edition. A short history of Crete, her people, and her ancient spiritual traditions. A mini-encyclopedia of the Minoan deities and the sacred symbols found in Minoan art. A full year's worth of seasonal rituals for the festivals in the Ariadne's Tribe sacred calendar. A lifetime's worth of rites of passage, from birth to death and beyond.

The Chalice and the Blade: Our History, Our Future by Riane Eisler. An insightful exploration of human culture from the viewpoint of dominator and partnership societies. Dr. Eisler uses the Minoans as an example of a partnership society, demonstrating the possibilities for peace, compassion, and a sharing economy that we may be able to replicate in our modern world.

The Dawn of Genius: The Minoan Super-Civilization and the Truth about Atlantis by Alan Butler. Don't be put off by the clickbait title. The first half of the book is up-to-date and accurate information about the Minoans, supported by current archaeology. The second half is educated guesses (in a historical and scientific manner, not a New Age-y manner) about Atlantis, the Phaistos disc, and some other unanswered questions about the Minoans.

The Goddesses and Gods of Old Europe by Marija Gimbutas. A classic work exploring the art and iconography of Old European (Neolithic) culture, with Minoan art as a continuation of Neolithic religion into the Bronze Age. Many of Dr. Gimbutas's theories that were once considered incorrect have recently been shown to be accurate thanks to hard archaeological evidence, much to the chagrin of the academic old guard.

Labrys & Horns: An Introduction to Modern Minoan Paganism by Laura Perry, second edition. The original, basic how-to book for inclusive modern Minoan spiritual practice. Includes symbols and practices, the pantheon, sacred calendar, daily devotionals and basic rituals you can use to begin or expand your relationship with the deities.

Lost Goddesses of Early Greece: A Collection of Pre-Hellenic Myths by Charlene Spretnak. Inspired recreations of what the early, pre-patriarchal myths in Greece and the Aegean might have looked like. This is an excellent source for what may be the original version of the Eleusinian Mysteries mythos cycle (the Demeter/Persephone tale) as it was known in ancient Crete.

Minotaur: Sir Arthur Evans and the Archaeology of the Minoan Myth by J.A. Macgillivray. This book is almost painfully honest about Sir Arthur Evans and his narrowminded Victorian mindset, including the racism (extreme even for his time) that caused him so many problems beginning even before he started excavating at Knossos. But it also gives an excellent description of Evans' lengthy excavations on Crete and his conclusions, many unsupported, which continue to bias archaeologists and historians to this day. It provides an enlightening description of the flourishing trade in faux Minoan artifacts that began almost as soon as the excavations started, and provides a reminder that Evans was almost single-handedly responsible for turning the Ashmolean Museum into the world-class institution it is today. Evans was a complicated man, neither a saint nor a monster, and his work had a profound and lasting impact.

O Mother Sun! A New View of the Cosmic Feminine by Patricia Monaghan. This is a review of sun goddesses from around the world and the changes that occurred as they were written out of mythology. The information in this book, along with some insightful dance ethnology research, allowed us to find Therasia and incorporate her into our pantheon.

The Riddle of the Labyrinth: The Quest to Crack an Ancient Code by Margalit Fox. The story of the decipherment of Linear B, including Alice Kober's important (and often ignored) contribution to the process. Her work was foundational to Michael Ventris' eventual success. Although Linear B was used to write Mycenaean Greek, not Minoan, the Linear B tablets from Knossos give us a window into the Minoan world during their final few centuries, under the Mycenaean occupation.

Bibliography

Anderson, Bonnie S. and Judith P. Zinsser. *A History of Their Own: Women in Europe from Prehistory to the Present*. Volume I. New York: Oxford University Press, 1999.

Bachofen, J.J. *Myth, Religion and Mother Right*. Princeton: Princeton University Press, 1967.

Barnes, Craig S. *In Search of the Lost Feminine: Decoding the Myths that Radically Reshaped Civilization*. Wheat Ridge, Colorado: Fulcrum Publishing, 2006.

Beard, Mary R. *Woman as Force in History*. London: Collier-Macmillan, 1946.

Betancourt, Philip P. *The History of Minoan Pottery*. Princeton, NJ: Princeton University Press, 1985.

Biers, William R. *The Archaeology of Greece: An Introduction*. Ithaca, NY: Cornell University Press, 1987.

Birtacha, Kiki, Eleni Asouti, Anastasia Deretzi, Dimitra Mylona, Anaya Sarpaki, and Katerina Trantalidou. "The Cooking Installations in Late Cycladic IA Akrotiri on Thera: The Case of the Kitchen in Pillar Pit 65, Preliminary Report." In *Horizon: A Colloquium on the Prehistory of the Cyclades*, edited by Neil Brodie, Jennifer Doole, Giorgios Gavalas, and Colin F. Renfrew, 25–28. Cambridge, UK: McDonald Institute for Archaeological Research, 2004.

Blomberg, Mary and Göran Henriksson. "Crossing Geographical Borders from Minoan Crete." In *Studies in Mediterranean Archaeology and Literature*, Pocket-book 173, edited by C. Gillis and B. Sjöberg, 191-210. Sävedalen: 2008.

————. "The Discovery of Minoan Astronomy and Its Debt to Robin Hägg." *Journal of Prehistoric Religion* 25, 64-77.

————. "The Function of the Minoan Oval House at Chamaizi." In *Archaeology and Ethnography. Papers from the annual meeting of SEAC (European Society for Astronomy in Culture)*, British

Archaeological Reports International Series 1647, edited by Emília Pásztor, 15-18. 2007.

_____. "Minoan Astronomy." In *Handbook of Archaeoastronomy and Ethnoastronomy*, edited by C.L.N. Ruggles, 1431-1441. New York: Springer, 2014.

_____. "Minoan Orientations in Context." In *Proceedings of the 9th Cretological Congress, Elounda (Crete)*, vol A4, edited by E. Tabakaki and A. Kaloutsakis, 319-331. Heraklion: 2006.

_____. "Orientations of the Minoan Palace at Phaistos in Crete." *Mediterranean Archaeology and Archaeometry*, Special Issue, Vol. 6, No. 3, 185-192. 2007.

_____. "Some Problems in Minoan Archaeoastronomy." In *Cosmic Catastrophes: a collection of articles, Proceedings of the European Society for Astronomy in Culture (SEAC)*, edited by M. Ktiva, I. Pustylnik, and L. Vesik, 15-22. Tartu: 2005.

Blomberg, Mary, Göran Henriksson and Maria Papathanassiou. "The Calendric Relationship between the Minoan Peak Sanctuary on Juktas and the Palace at Knossos." In *Astronomy of Ancient Societies. Proceedings of the Conference "Astronomy of Ancient Civilizations" of the European Society for Astronomy (SEAC) associated with the Joint European and National Astronomical Meeting (JENAM), Moscow, May 23-27, 2000*, 82-91. Edited by T.M. Potyomkina and V.N. Obridko. 2002.

Blomberg, Peter E. "Malady or Vanity: a Minoan Peak Sanctuary Figurine." In *Ancient Cosmologies and Modern Prophets. Proceedings of the 20th Conference of the European Society for Astronomy in Culture*. Anthropological Notebooks 19, supplement, edited by Ivan Sprajc and Peter Pehani, 121-128. Ljubljana: Slovene Anthropological Society, 2013.

Boulding, Elise. *The Underside of History*. Boulder, Colorado: Westview Press, 1976.

Bulfinch, Thomas. *Bulfinch's Mythology: The Age of Fable*. Garden City, New York: Doubleday and Company, Inc., 1968.

Butler, Alan. *The Dawn of Genius: The Minoan Super-Civilization and the Truth about Atlantis*. London: Watkins Publishing, 2014.

Campbell, Joseph. *The Hero With a Thousand Faces*. Bollinger Series. Princeton: Princeton University Press, 1973.

————. *The Masks of God*. Vol. I-IV. New York: Penguin Books, 1977.

————. *Myths to Live By*. New York: Penguin Books, 1972.

————. *Primitive Mythology*. New York: Penguin Books, 1985.

Carignano, Micaela. "Reconstructing Minoan Dining Practice and Sociopolitical Organization in Neopalatial Households and Palaces." PhD dissertation, Department of Classics, Cornell University, Ithaca, New York, 2018. Accessed 27 February 2024. https://ecommons.cornell.edu/server/api/core/bitstreams/545fe8fb-e681-4436-b158-6ef17d0b0992/content

Castleden, Rodney. *Minoans: Life in Bronze Age Crete*. London: Routledge, 1993.

Chadwick, John. *The Decipherment of Linear B*. Cambridge: Cambridge University Press, 1998.

Chadwick, John. *Reading the Past: Linear B and Related Scripts*. Berkeley and Los Angeles: University of California Press, 1997.

Charles River Editors. *The Minoans and Mycenaeans: The History of the Civilizations that First Developed Ancient Greek Culture*. Charles River Editors, 2016.

Cline, Eric H. *1177 B.C.: The Year Civilization Collapsed*. Turning Points in Ancient History. Princeton, NJ: Princeton University Press, 2021.

Durdin-Robertson, Lawrence. *The Symbolism of Temple Architecture*. Enniscorthy, County Wexford, United Kingdom: Cesara Publications, 1978.

Eliade, Mircea. *Patterns in Comparative Religion*. Sheed & Ward, 1958.

————. *Rites and Symbols of Initiation*. New York: Harper & Row, 1958.

Eisler, Riane. *The Chalice and the Blade: Our History, Our Future.* San Francisco: HarperOne, 1988.

Evans, Arthur. *The Palace of Minos: A Comparative Account of the Successive Stages of the Early Cretan Civilization as Illustrated by the Discoveries at Knossos.* Vol. 1. London: Macmillan and Company, Ltd., 1921.

Evans, Arthur. *The Palace of Minos: A Comparative Account of the Successive Stages of the Early Cretan Civilization as Illustrated by the Discoveries at Knossos.* Vol. 2. London: Macmillan and Company, Ltd., 1928.

Evans, Arthur. *The Palace of Minos: A Comparative Account of the Successive Stages of the Early Cretan Civilization as Illustrated by the Discoveries at Knossos.* Vol. 3. London: Macmillan and Company, Ltd., 1930.

Evans, Arthur. *The Palace of Minos: A Comparative Account of the Successive Stages of the Early Cretan Civilization as Illustrated by the Discoveries at Knossos.* Vol. 4. London: Macmillan and Company, Ltd., 1935.

Fox, Margalit. *The Riddle of the Labyrinth: The Quest to Crack an Ancient Code.* New York: Ecco Press, 2014.

Freely, John. *Crete.* New York: New Amsterdam Books, 1988.

Friedrich, Walter L. *Fire in the Sea: The Santorini Volcano: Natural History and the Legend of Atlantis.* Cambridge: Cambridge University Press, 2000.

Gimbutas, Marija. *The Goddesses and Gods of Old Europe: Myths and Cult Images.* Berkeley: University of California Press, 1974.

Goodison, Lucy. "From Tholos Tomb to Throne Room: Perceptions of the Sun in Minoan Ritual." *Aegeum*, vol. 22: 77-95. 2001.

Gore, Belinda. *Ecstatic Body Postures: An Alternate Reality Workbook.* Santa Fe, New Mexico: Bear and Company, 1995.

Graham, James Walter. *The Palaces of Crete.* Princeton, New Jersey: Princeton University Press, 1987.

Guthrie, W.K.C. *The Greeks and Their Gods.* Boston: Beacon Press, 1955.

Hamilton, Edith. *Mythology*. New York: The New American Library, Mentor Edition, 1969.

Harissis, Anastasios V. and Haralampos V. Harissis. *Apiculture in the Prehistoric Aegean: Minoan and Mycenaean Symbols Revisited*. Oxford: British Archaeological Reports Ltd., 2009.

Henriksson, Göran and Mary Blomberg. "Summary of the Archaeoastronomical Study of Minoan Sites." In *Proceedings of the 11th Cretological Congress, Rethymno (Crete), 21-27 October 2011*, vol A1.1. Edited by Eirene Tavilaki, 153-171. Rethymno: 2018.

_____. "Petsophas and the Summer Solstice." *Opuscula Atheniensia* 22-23, 147-151. Athens, Greece: Swedish Institute at Athens, 1998.

Higgins, Reynold. *The Archaeology of Minoan Crete*. New York: Henry Z. Walck, Inc., 1973.

_____. *Minoan and Mycenaean Art*. London: Thames & Hudson, 1997.

Isaakidou, Valasia. "Cooking in the Labyrinth: Exploring 'cuisine' at Bronze Age Knossos." In *Cooking Up the Past: Food and culinary practices in the Neolithic and Bronze Age Aegean*, edited by Christopher Mee and Josette Renard. Oxford, UK: Oxbow Books, 2007.

Jung, Carl G. *Man and His Symbols*. New York: Doubleday & Co., 1964.

Kerenyi, Carl. *Dionysos: Archetypal Image of Indestructible Life*. Princeton, New Jersey: Princeton University Press, 1996.

Konsola, Dora. Trans. Alexandra Doumas. *Crete: Knossos, Phaistos, Aghia Triada, Gortyn, Malia, Zakros, Gournia, Herakleion Museum, Aghias Nikolaos Museum, Chania Museum*. Athens: John Decopoulos, 1983.

Kyriakidis, Evangelos. "Unidentified floating objects on Minoan seals." *American Journal of Archaeology* 109 (2): 137-154, 2005.

Lapatin, Kenneth. *Mysteries of the Snake Goddess: Art, Desire, and the Forging of History*. Boston: Houghton Mifflin Harcourt, 2002.

Leach, Maria, ed. *Standard Dictionary of Folklore, Mythology, and Legend.* New York: Funk & Wagnalls Co., 1950.

Leeming, David Adams. *The World of Myth.* New York: Oxford University Press, 1990.

Macgillivray, Joseph Alexander. *Minotaur: Sir Arthur Evans and the Archaeology of the Minoan Myth.* New York: Hill and Wang, 2000.

Marinatos, Nanno. *Akrotiri, Thera, and the East Mediterranean.* Athens, Greece: Militos Editions, 2015.

_____. *Minoan Kingship and the Solar Goddess: A Near Eastern Koine.* Champaign: University of Illinois Press, 2010.

_____. *Minoan Religion: Ritual, Image, and Symbol.* Columbia, South Carolina: University of South Carolina Press, 1993.

McEnroe, John C. *Architecture of Minoan Crete: Constructing Identity in the Aegean Bronze Age.* Austin: University of Texas Press, 2010.

Monaghan, Patricia. *Book of Goddesses and Heroines.* New York: Dutton, 1981.

_____. *O Mother Sun! A New View of the Cosmic Feminine.* Freedom, California: The Crossing Press, 1994.

Morgan, Lyvia. *The Miniature Wall Paintings of Thera: A Study in Aegean Culture and Iconography.* Cambridge, UK: Cambridge University Press, 1988.

Nilsson, M.P. *Minoan-Mycenaean Religion.* Cambridge, UK: Cambridge University Press, 1950.

_____. *The Mycenaean Origin of Greek Mythology.* Cambridge, UK: Cambridge University Press, 1932.

Noble, Vicki. *The Double Goddess: Women Sharing Power.* Rochester, Vermont: Bear and Company, 2003.

O'Brien, Cormac. *The Fall of Empires: From Glory to Ruin, an Epic Account of History's Ancient Civilizations.* New York: Fall River Press, 2009.

Papageorgiou, Irini. "Stories of Coming of Age at prehistoric Akrotiri. Rituals and iconographic correlations." *ΑΛΣ*

(Periodical Publication of the Society for the Promotion of Studies on Prehistoric Thera) 8: 26-111, 2011.

Pomeroy, Sarah B. *Goddesses, Whores, Wives, and Slaves: Women in Classical Antiquity*. New York: Schocken Books, 1975.

Rethemiotakis, Georgios. "The "Divine Couple" Ring from Poros and the Origins of the Minoan Calendar." *Mitteilungen Des Deutschen Archäologischen Instituts Athenische Abteilung* 131: 1-29, 2016.

Sapouna-Sakellaraki, Efi. *Zominthos: A mountain palace*. Athens, Greece: The Psycha Foundation, 2022.

Sjoo, Monica, and Barbara Mor. *The Great Cosmic Mother: Rediscovering the Religion of the Earth*. San Francisco: Harper & Row, 1987.

Spretnak, Charlene. *Lost Goddesses of Early Greece: A Collection of Pre-Hellenic Myths*. Boston: Beacon Press, 1992.

Stone, Merlin. *When God Was a Woman*. New York: Prentice Hall Press, 1982.

Straffon, Cheryl and Lana Jarvis. *The Goddess in Crete: A Guide to 100 Minoan and Other Sites*. Penzance, Cornwall: Meyn Mamvro Publications: 2015.

Vandenberg, Philipp. *The Mystery of the Oracles*. New York: Macmillan Publishing Co., Inc.

Vaughan, Agnes Carr. *The House of the Double Axe: The Palace at Knossos*. Garden City, New York: Doubleday and Company, Inc., 1959.

Warren, Peter. *The Aegean Civilizations*. New York: Peter Bedrick Books, 1989.

Wunderlich, Hans Georg. Trans. Richard Winston. *The Secret of Crete*. Athens, Greece: 1983.

About the Author

Laura Perry is an artist and author, and the founder and Temple Mom of Ariadne's Tribe, a worldwide inclusive Minoan spiritual tradition. The Minoans of Bronze Age Crete have been a passion of hers since a fateful art history class introduced her to the colorful frescoes of ancient Knossos way back in high school. In addition to her work with the Tribe, Laura is a third degree Wiccan priestess, a Reiki master, and a longtime herbalist. Her previous books about Tribe spirituality include *Labrys & Horns: An Introduction to Modern Minoan Paganism* and *Ariadne's Thread: Awakening the Wonders of the Ancient Minoans in Our Modern Lives*, both now in second edition. She has also written a Minoan historical novel *(The Last Priestess of Malia)* and a Minoan-themed mm romance *(Leap! A Love Story)* as well as *The Minoan Coloring Book* and *The Minoan Tarot*. When she's not busy drawing, writing, or leading rituals and workshops, you can probably find her digging in the garden or giving a living history demonstration at a local historic site. You can find her online at LauraPerryAuthor.com, where you can find links to all her social media, including her YouTube channel with its Ariadne's Tribe playlist.

Other Books in the *Pantheon* Series

The Egyptians
Robin Herne
978-1-78535-504-2 (Paperback)
978-1-78535-505-9 (e-book)

The Greeks
Irisanya Moon
978-1-78535-506-6 (Paperback)
978-1-78535-507-3 (e-book)

The Irish
Morgan Daimler
978-1-80341-649-6 (Paperback)
978-1-80341-648-9 (e-book)

The Norse
Morgan Daimler
978-1-78904-141-5 (Paperback)
978-1-78904-142-2 (e-book)

The Romans
Rachel Roberts
978-1-80341-682-3 (Paperback)
978-1-80341-930-5 (e-book)

The Welsh
Mhara Starling
978-1-80341-742-4 (Paperback)
978-1-80341-741-7 (e-book)

Readers of ebooks can buy or view any of these bestsellers by clicking on the live link in the title. Most titles are published in paperback and as an ebook. Paperbacks are available in traditional bookshops. Both print and ebook formats are available online.

Find more titles and sign up to our readers' newsletter
www.collectiveinkbooks.com/paganism

For video content, author interviews and more, please subscribe to our YouTube channel.

MoonBooksPublishing

Follow us on social media for book news, promotions and more:

Facebook: Moon Books

Instagram: @MoonBooksCI

X: @MoonBooksCI

TikTok: @MoonBooksCI